Blessed Be

Blessed Be

Discover unexpected blessings, divine
favor, and kingdom purpose

FOR MOMS OF
SPECIAL NEEDS CHILDREN

Bethany Thomas

gatekeeper press

Columbus, Ohio

BLESSED BE: DISCOVER UNEXPECTED BLESSINGS,
DIVINE FAVOR, AND KINGDOM PURPOSE FOR MOMS
OF SPECIAL NEEDS CHILDREN

Published by Gatekeeper Press
2167 Stringtown Rd, Suite 109
Columbus, OH 43123-2989
www.GatekeeperPress.com

ISBN 9781642376104

Cover Design by Chelsi Van Slyke

Printed in the United States of America

"Blessed are the poor in spirit, for theirs is the kingdom of heaven.

Blessed are those who mourn, for they shall be comforted.

Blessed are the meek, for they shall inherit the earth.

Blessed are those who hunger and thirst for righteousness, for they shall be filled.

Blessed are the merciful, for they shall obtain mercy.

Blessed are the pure in heart, for they shall see God.

Blessed are the peacemakers, for they shall be called sons of God.

Blessed are those who are persecuted for righteousness' sake, for theirs is the kingdom of heaven."

Matthew 5:3-12 (NKJV)

This book is dedicated to...

ALMIGHTY GOD! If it weren't for God's endless grace, mercy, protection, and provision, this book would not have come to fruition. I give ALL the glory to our Lord and Savior, JESUS CHRIST.

To my husband, RANDY THOMAS, and our two beautiful children, MADDIE and JAKE. Randy, you've sacrificed so much to provide a beautiful, blessed life for "Team Thomas." I pray that I can honor, love, and support you as selflessly as you have for us. I love you so much and can't wait to grow old and wrinkly together.

To the women of Majestic Church, this journey began when I walked into a home filled with women I'd never met, but was predestined to do life with. Thank you to my spiritual moms - LAURA KNOWLTON, CHRISTY OZEE, LAURA MACK, KELLY LYMAN, KIM SAWLER, LESLIE FLUEGEL (OUR ANGEL), CYNDI GREEN, JOY NICHTER, VANESSA NOLAN, TRACY ZOZOYA, TESSA MCCALL, SUMMER MILLER, MARY BELLINGER, LINDA (AND TRACEY) SHARPE, MARIA BUTLER HILL, LISA HUGHES, ELLEN TEALL, D'ANI PULLAM, ELIZABETH LANE, JODI GAIL, CAROLE NELSON, AND ANDREA MCCRACKEN. This work was birthed through the Experiencing God Bible study but my journey began with you all in The Armor of God. My love for you, the prayer warriors of Majestic Church, is indescribable...

To the special moms and sisters in Christ who I get to do life with each week, and who I did this study of The Beatitudes with when it was held together by a staple and typos throughout. YOU ladies are my reason, my purpose, my drive, my inspiration, and my heroes. REBECCA LABINE, you are my other half in this ministry and I can't wait to serve Jesus together until our last breath on earth. My Team on Tuesday mornings—NANCY OLIVER, KAITY MARCOS, ANASTASIA SINGLETON, KATHERINE ARBEEN,

ASHLEY BOZARTH, TIFFANI MENDEZ, LOURDES RAHN, RHONDA PAGEL, MANDY MORRISON AND ALL HER MAMA'S, TARITA WALKER, LACY WILLIAMS, CAMMIE BELL, AND THE BEAUTIFUL CHRISTY KIRKLAND. Team Wednesday home group—SAMANTHA KELLEY, ALANNA BROWN, TAMARA HITT, KRISTEN GRENIER, LUCIANA GALLOWAY, NANCY CASTILLO, AND SUSAN KEARNEY. Love me summa you, ladies!

I want to thank my family, DAVID (my daddy and ultimate HERO) and ANDRA HOUSE, STEPHANIE AND JEFF BIELMAN, AND LAUREN HOUSE, I love you all so much more than words can say. Mom, Dale House, I know you're never far away and I can feel your presence in this project from Heaven. I miss and love you so much. MIKE and LINDA THOMAS, we love you more than you'll ever know. LISA and RICHARD PEREZ, we love you and can't wait to get you back to Texas!

Last but NOT least - My spiritual dad and his beautiful wife, MIKE AND SUSAN ROBERTS…" thank you" is not sufficient in expressing my gratitude for you both. Your encouragement, selfless work for this ministry, and above all else, I am grateful for your fervent prayers over the years for my family. You are Shepherds for the Kingdom!

Introduction

I'm going to let you in on a little secret: WE'RE ALL SPECIAL NEEDS CHILDREN OF GOD. That's right! Each and every one of us walking on planet earth has needs that no one else does. We're all in recovery from something. Although I wrote this Bible study for moms whose children have physical and developmental delays and/or disabilities, let me tell you that every home has difficulties and struggles that disables happiness. When you see "special need" or "disability", mentally insert which applies to you—addiction, depression, infidelity, anger, illness, etc. Regardless the need, Jesus, and ONLY JESUS, is able to do far more, exceedingly above and beyond all you could ever ask or imagine (Ephesians 3:20).

I pray that you allow God to breathe new life into your journey in the coming weeks as He reveals His promises for you through His Word. My hope is that, by spending time with Jesus in this study of The Beatitudes, you become consumed by a Holy Fire, igniting a hunger and thirst for His presence like never before. As He manifests Himself, you will be beautifully undone by a greater understanding as to why He chose you to be the mother of His most fragile, precious children.

You were created for this very important role and it's God's love and complete trust in *you* that sets you apart. God doesn't call those who are equipped for this kind of Kingdom work—He calls those who He desires to equip by entering into a real, tangible, intimate love relationship. With Jesus beside you, He will supernaturally shift your focus and stir your heart to celebrate the divine role He's placed you in.

Being a mom is hard work. The work is even harder when your children have special needs that differ from other families. As you begin this study, pray and ask God to prepare your heart to be emptied of self, making room for your spirit to be overflowing with the love of Jesus.

Blessings and love,
Bethany Thomas

About This Study

"The Beatitudes" are blessings taught by Jesus in the Sermon on the Mount in the Gospel of Matthew. The Beatitudes are spoken in two parts: the CONDITION and the RESULT.

With each Beatitude, Jesus preaches new meanings to the Old Testament way of life by revealing that people who are perceived as "unfortunate" are the ones truly "blessed." Jesus teaches that the unpromising circumstances for people who are suffering are what actually make them promisingly favored by God. Beatitude derives from the Greek word for "HAPPINESS," "Happy are those who . . ."

In an excerpt from his series, AN EXPOSITION OF THE GOSPEL OF MATTHEW, Dr. Allen Ross provides a greater understanding regarding the Greek translation and deeper meaning of "happy." He states,

> "Perhaps it would be helpful at the beginning to deal briefly with this word 'blessed.' There is a desire today to translate the word with 'happy'. But that does not seem to capture all that is intended here in the text, primarily because modern usage of the word 'happy' has devalued it. This term is an exclamation of the inner joy and peace that comes with being right with God. Happiness may indeed be a part of it; but it is a happiness that transcends what happens in the world around us, a happiness that comes to the soul from being favored by God. That is why it can call for rejoicing under intense persecution. In some ways the Lord's declaration of 'blessed' is a pledge of divine reward for the inner spiritual character of the righteous; in other ways it is His description of the spiritual attitude and state of people who are right with God." Dr. Ross goes on to say, "So when Jesus says 'blessed are they,' He is not only describing them as being filled with an inner sense of joy and

peace because they are right with God, but He is praising them for their character and pledging divine rewards for it."

As you dig deeper into this study, God will pour His favor into every crevice of your being—mind, body, and soul. You will gain as much as your willing to give. By putting effort and work into this Bible study, you will experience freedom and victory. You will celebrate the position He's chosen for you as a mom whose Kingdom Purpose is so specific, that you'll never question His love for you again. The moment you discover what He can do in you, you'll never doubt Him again. Blessed are you . . .

HOMEWORK assignments are very easy and are meant to grow your relationship with Jesus. As a mom of two special needs children, I totally "get it" when time isn't always guaranteed. The homework is just for you and Jesus; however, I feel like it would be a powerful way of sharing in the group what that Lord revealed to you throughout the week regarding your time with Him. DO NOT feel like the homework has to be completed in order to attend group! The lessons are the main focus of group time. The extra time in prayer and the Word is a bonus blessing for each of you individually.

JOURNAL & PRAYER TIME is crucial to developing a love relationship with Jesus. Read the scripture I've provided per day for 5 days, re-writing each one in your own words. Journal throughout the day all of your thoughts, fears, emotions, highs, and lows for the day. This time with the Lord is meant to bring you closer to Him and in the Word daily. If you don't understand the context of the scripture, I recommend starting at the beginning of that particular chapter, or at least 5 verses that precede it. The Message Bible is also a huge help! It's written in today's terms, making it much easier to wrap your head around.

SUGGESTIONS

- Download the You Version Bible app. It's free and available in iTunes, Google Play, and Android Market.

- Keep notes as you go, you'll be amazed at the impact God will make on your heart and home throughout this study.

- Stay in contact with one another throughout the week. Also, choose one day a month to meet for fellowship and breaking bread. We easily isolate ourselves and the enemy uses that as a way to keep us under his control. Even if it's coffee and biscuits, girl time is a blessing.

Lesson 1

Blessed are the poor in spirit,
For theirs is the kingdom of Heaven.

Matthew 5:3

The poverty of one's spirit is a prerequisite to acquiring the other Beatitudes. Without totally surrendering pride, control, sin, and self-sufficiency, it is impossible to rely on God. Once we're empty of everything—self, circumstance, control, earthly desires and possessions we covet—then we are perfectly positioned to be filled. Why? Because God cannot fill what is full.

There are hundreds of scriptures in the Bible that tell us how God and His Son, Jesus Christ, were saving, healing, defending, and blessing those who sought God above all else. Being "poor in spirit" can't be faked; complete humility and selflessness are what draws God closer to those who desperately want to be in His presence.

THE CONDITION

When Jesus describes the blessed as being "poor" in spirit, He is not referring to their financial status. He is speaking about emptiness in their spirit after pouring everything out in prayer and repentance to God. The condition of those He says are uniquely blessed is their poverty of spirit. Characteristics of someone who is POOR IN SPIRIT:

- The spiritually poor have a keen awareness of their sinfulness and are eager to repent; their need for God's grace is ever present. READ Psalms 51:1-3.

- A person who is poor in spirit has total awareness that they cannot save themselves, nor do they have the ability to glorify themselves according to God. READ James 1:2-5.

- A person who sees blessings in that they are finite (limited) and God is infinite (He has no limits). READ Psalm 147:5.

- Glory is always given to God, never taking credit for the blessings He's bestowed upon them. READ Luke 14:11.

God created you and I to seek Him in all things. God created life in order to build His Kingdom. The greatest desire of God's heart is that we love Him first; not even our children are to be higher on our list of priorities than God. I know that may sound crazy and I understand why. You might think to yourself, "If God wanted to be first in my life then why did He give me a child whose life is literally dependent on me? I'm so exhausted that I can hardly think straight 99 percent of the time! I don't have anything more to give. My time is devoted to caring for my child and my marriage is hanging on by a thread. I can barely make room for laundry! Now this woman says God wants me to prioritize HIM? How on earth can I do that with everything I'm up against on a daily basis?"

I have been there. I thought I was honoring God by putting my children first, but I was exhausted and full of resentment. When I began growing my relationship with Jesus, I found out that I wasn't expected to do anything more than accept His love for me. He was the giver, I was the one receiving love and comfort. As I began loving Jesus, I understood who God created me to be—His daughter.

When Jesus is the rock that you stand upon, He is the one you prioritize. Jesus is the most giving, loving, patient person in my life. Because I place Him above anyone or anything, my love for others has changed. Through my unwavering love for Jesus, God was able to open my heart to love my family fully and unconditionally. Without loving the Lord more than anyone else, it will be impossible for you to tap into a fervent, passionate, perfect love for your family.

1. What area(s) of your life have changed the most since having your special child?

2. Since becoming a special mom, what are some personal changes you've experienced where you can see God has been working within you?

READ PHILIPPIANS 3:8.

1. What did Paul consider a loss?

2. What did Paul gain?

3. Does Paul seem to miss the life he had before gaining a life with Jesus Christ?

4. If there are areas of your past life that you struggle to let go of, write them down in the space below. Then, begin asking the Holy Spirit to show you the unexpected blessings you've gained since becoming a mom. Be honest in this exercise, you're only going to grow by digging deep. Besides, God already knows your heart, and He's waited a long time for this moment.

_____

_____

_____

_____

_____

_____

_____

If we are to count everything as a loss, renouncing what we once thought meant so much to us, then we have to make a choice. This is a crucial step in embracing your inability to change your circumstances. The choice you and I must make is this: choosing Christ <u>or</u> everything else. God may not have caused the pain and sadness you suffer, or the pain your child suffers, but He will USE them for His glory. Holding on to the emotional and spiritual weakness in your soul, you're full. By releasing everything that holds you down, you're making room for God to reside deep within your spirit. Circle the emotions below that you contend with.

ANXIETY   FEAR   RESENTMENT   EXHAUSTION   DOUBT
CONFUSION   ANGER   FRUSTRATION   DENIAL   BITTER
GRATEFUL   HOPEFUL   OVERWHELMED   NUMB

In order to count all things as loss, we must empty ourselves of ourselves and everything that encompasses self. In doing this, we will draw near to Jesus in the silence. We will let go of what doesn't matter, and begin to thrive on *who* does—Jesus. This is the way Paul lived his Apostolic life after meeting Jesus in the desert on the way to Damascus. When Jesus dwells within you, you'll know it by the supernatural peace you feel, even in the seasons of emptiness.

READ PHILIPPIANS 3:17, then WRITE it in your own words below

_____

_____

_____

_____

_____

There are hundreds of scriptures in the Bible that tell us how God and His Son, Jesus Christ, were saving, healing, defending, and blessing those who sought God above all else. Being "poor in spirit" can't be faked; complete humility and selflessness are what draws God closer to those who desperately want to be in His presence.

I can honestly say that I would have never been desperate for God's presence in my life if it weren't for my children. I never would've believed I'd be a good enough mom to have special needs children. No way! The role as a special need mommy is a HUGE responsibility and I was a pretty irresponsible person before having kids. I was selfish, concerned with my social life above all else. But God created me to seek Him in all things and build His Kingdom, therefore He blessed me with a future that would leave no room for a social life…and I thank Him every single day for that.

THE RESULT

Those who are poor in spirit, the people who live empty of self and sin, are blessed with the Kingdom of Heaven. Are you wondering what Jesus means when He says the "Kingdom of Heaven" belongs to the poor in spirit? In Theology, they refer to it as *the already and not yet*; the sense of "the Kingdom was brought forth through grace" and "the Kingdom of Heaven that will be when Jesus returns."

In other words, the kingdom of Heaven is yours now and forever. You don't have to wait to experience the gift God has for you! God's blessings are pouring over us in our present reality and even more blessings are to come. Healing is promised to those who love the Lord. Healing was something Jesus did over and over again in His ministry.

Jesus preached Beatitudes in two different sermons, the Sermon on the Mount in the Gospel of Matthew and the Sermon on the Plains in the Gospel of Luke. Both sermons were preceded by miraculous work. Let's explore this a little further. There is a beautiful parallel between these sermons that goes way beyond the Beatitudes spoken.

READ MATTHEW 4:23 through 5:3.

1.   Where was Jesus positioned?

2.   Who was healed before His sermon began?

READ LUKE 6:17-19:

1.   Where was Jesus positioned?

2.   Who was healed before His sermon began?

As Jesus looks upon the crowd of people, many of whom had been suffering in sickness, others tortured by mental illness that the enemy inflicted upon them, He began to heal them simply by the power of God within Him.

Jesus *"**went up** on the mountain and His disciples came to Him"* in Matthew but *"**came down** with them and stood on a level place"* in Luke. There will be days that you feel as if Jesus is sitting at a distance, unsure if He's hearing your prayers. There are going to be seasons where the silence from unanswered prayers creates doubt in your innermost being. There will be days and seasons where you feel Him moving powerfully, witness His supernatural presence of the Holy Spirit that leaves you undone and thirsting for more. Circumstances and seasons change but we will never face the storms alone. We can stand on this promise God made, *"Never will I leave you; never will I forsake you."* *(Hebrews 13:5)*

Jesus was healing everyone who was physically, emotionally, and spiritually broken who'd come to Him! *Everyone* who followed Jesus, believed He was who He said He was, submitted themselves to Him, emptying themselves and coming to Him in desperation and brokenness were HEALED!

Once they were healed, Jesus teaches them that **their poverty of spirit was a promotion**! Because of their FAITH IN JESUS in the midst of such brutal suffering, they were healed forever, on earth and in Heaven.

Jesus hasn't changed. The reason we must be poor in spirit before embarking on the next few weeks of this Beatitudes study is this: unless we are empty, there is no room for God. Our nothingness is the beginning of experiencing everything God has in store for us. Give everything God takes without hesitation and take everything God gives with complete humility and thanksgiving to Him. In doing so, you will understand what Paul meant in 2 Corinthians 6:10. WRITE it below.

_____

_____

_____

_____

_____

_____

I promise you that your child will be healed. I can't tell you whether the healing will be here on earth, but I can promise you THEY WILL BE HEALED. If the healing comes once they're in Heaven, then it is my obligation to plead with you to get in right standing with God. Accept Jesus Christ as your Lord and Savior and give your life to God. What you're unable to witness your child accomplish on earth, you'll see in the Kingdom of Heaven! What does that look like for your family? Is your prayer to see your child run, skip, hop, jump, or swim? Is it to hear them laugh, cry, enjoy silence or contentment, or to hear that sweet child say, "Mama"?

You will. I promise. God created your child for His glory and to grow the Kingdom. Please, don't risk missing out on the perfection awaiting your child through the grace of Jesus Christ.

WRITE JOHN 5:30 below.

_____

_____

_____

_____

_____

_____

DISCUSSION

1. What is the Holy Spirit saying to you through this lesson?

2. Have you ever considered your emotional and physical emptiness to be an invitation from God to rely on Him in a more intimate way?

3. Is there someone in your life you've admired because of their selfless service of others?

4. What does it mean to you to have hope?

5. Is Jesus Christ your Lord and Savior? If not, please ask the Lord to come into your heart. If you're not already a member of a women's group Bible study or church, I pray that you will reach out to the friend or family member who's invited you in the past.

BLESSESD ARE YOU

who are empty of self and sin,

for yours is The Kingdom of *grace* here,

and the Kingdom of *glory* hereafter.

Every week you will have five days of homework. The homework won't take long but it will keep you in the Word and hold you accountable to spend time with the Lord. Read each scripture provided, then re-write it, and journal what the Holy Spirit is saying to you through the scripture. Write the dates down as well, it's a great way of remembering the season you were in at the time. Going back and seeing the answered and unanswered prayers will impact you along the way. Unanswered prayers are often the most life-changing.

DAY 1

LUKE 14:33

_____

_____

_____

_____

_____

_____

_____

_____

_____

_____

_____

_____

_____

DAY 2

MATTHEW 13:44

_____

_____

_____

_____

_____

_____

_____

_____

_____

_____

_____

_____

_____

_____

DAY 3

ISAIAH 55:8

_____

_____

_____

_____

_____

_____

_____

_____

_____

_____

_____

_____

_____

_____

DAY 4

PSALM 28:7

_____

_____

_____

_____

_____

_____

_____

_____

_____

_____

_____

_____

_____

_____

_____

_____

_____

DAY 5

LUKE 6:24

_____

_____

_____

_____

_____

_____

_____

_____

_____

_____

_____

_____

_____

Lesson 2

Blessed are those who mourn,
for they will be comforted.

Matthew 5:4

Last week we learned that the Kingdom of Heaven is ours now (through Grace) and in the hereafter (when Jesus comes again). This week is different in that the promise of comfort and laughter will be felt in the future—after the mourning is over. This doesn't necessarily mean that we will have to wait long to receive God's comfort when we're devastated; the circumstances surrounding the mourning determines when His comfort begins, not the mourning itself.

Merriam-Webster Dictionary defines "mourning" as

1. The act of sorrowing

2. An outward sign of grief for a person's death

3. A period of time during which signs of grief are shown

THE CONDITION

The condition this week is that of mourning. Mourning indicates pain, grief and brokenness over loss, usually the death of a loved one. The loss of a valued life that's gone astray, wandering in darkness, unleashes a deep mourning on those who love them. Bankruptcy, divorce, and declining health are other examples of life-altering events where loss is felt on a different level, but no less a casualty. For many special parents like you and me, the diagnosis can feel like the onset of a long, drawn out, unrelenting death over and over again.

Isaiah 61 is just some of the many prophetic words about Jesus, spoken by God's prophet, Isaiah. These words and visions were given to him hundreds of years before Jesus was born. The people living in the time of the Old Testament were under the Law of God, strict rules to abide by. It wasn't until Jesus died for us on the cross that salvation was even an option for entering into eternal life. God's Hebrew people had been enslaved and under attack for generations, but God used Isaiah to preach hope to the broken, mournful people.

READ Isaiah 61:1-2

1. Isaiah was given the gift of prophesy to preach what? To whom?

2. Who will be healed?

3. Of those who mourn, who will be comforted?

WRITE Isaiah 61:3 below. Underline the words that speak into your spirit.

_____

_____

_____

_____

_____

People mourn in seasons of trial and tribulation, but what if the anguish Jesus is referring to in the Matthew 5:4 and Luke 6:21 is the result of sin? You might dismiss this possibility because something about hearing Jesus say "blessed are those who sin" just feels wrong and completely out of alignment with God's teachings. This statement isn't written anywhere in the Bible, is it?

READ Luke 7:36

1. Where was Jesus invited? Who invited Him?

2. What did the woman do to Jesus?

3. What do you know about her based on the details in this scripture?

We don't know much about her other than her emotional state and what Simon the Pharisee said about her, calling her a "sinner." Her gentle gestures toward Jesus say more about her than anything else at this point; her actions are filled with purpose to honor and dignify Jesus.

When sitting down for a meal with invited guests in Jesus' time, formal procedures were strictly followed. These procedures had been in place since Old Testament times, beginning when God and His two Angels visited Abraham and Sarah in Genesis 18:3-6. These procedures were well known and nothing new to Simon the Pharisee, the host of this dinner. They are listed below:

1. Upon arriving for the meal, the host would first greet their guest with a verbal blessing such as, "Peace be with you."

2. Second, there was a formal kiss where they'd place hands on each other's shoulders, pulling together and giving a kiss, first on the right cheek then the left.

3. Next, a servant would immediately remove the guest's sandals to ensure dirt from their shoes wouldn't be brought in. The dirt from unpaved streets and pathways would ruin any flooring in the house, defiling the home. Removing the shoes was done to show consideration and respect for the homeowner and for God.

4. Once their shoes were off, the guest's feet were washed by a servant who would pour water over their feet, rubbing them gently with their hands, and drying them with a towel.

5. After that, the guest's head was anointed with olive oil scented with spices.

6. The final formality was to give the guest a cool drink of water, indicating the guest was worthy of being received in peace and as a show of friendship.

In Luke 7:39 Simon the Pharisee *saw what the woman was doing to Jesus, he thought to himself, "If this man were a prophet, He would know who and what sort of person this woman is who is touching Him, that she is a 'sinner."* Jesus heard Simon's thoughts and immediately replies with the Parable of Two Debtors.

READ Luke 7:40-43. In this parable, Jesus represents the forgiving creditor and the debts represent sin.

1. Who do you think represents the one who owes 50 denarii?

2. Who do you think represents the one who owes the larger amount of 500 denarii?

3. Who does the Pharisee say will love and appreciate the forgiveness of their debt more?

The Pharisee easily answered Jesus' question and probably thought nothing about it at first. Jesus, on the other hand was making a point with this parable. The judgmental persecution Simon is inflicting on this woman who is visibly repentant, desperate for peace and an end to her brokenness, is about to be called out for what it is: total hypocrisy.

READ Luke 7:44-50. WRITE verse 50 below.

_____

_____

_____

_____

_____

For Simon, sin was what caused this woman to be held captive and he didn't care that she was hurting. He saw a woman who - in his opinion - deserved to be tortured by her pain. Jesus knew that by repenting and living a new life as a Christian, this precious woman would be able to live life with joy. Her CONDITION was that she was in mourning; the RESULT was the comfort of Jesus right then and there.

Simon tried to expose Jesus as being a false prophet for allowing such an immoral woman to touch him. Simon *purposely* failed to follow centuries-old formal procedure when Jesus arrived at his dinner by invitation. Simon never intended to honor Jesus; his motives were most likely to humiliate the Messiah by NOT following Jewish customs that night. Jesus, by hearing Simon's thoughts and answering him out loud must've left the Pharisee speechless.

THE RESULT

The Bible tells us little about this woman other than she was a sinner (or "immoral" in other translations). Jesus points out that her sins were many, similar to others in the Bible who mourned sin, such as

- The Samaritan woman at the well (John 4:7-38) who lived in shame and isolation. Yet, when Jesus comforts her without being asked, her life was forever changed.

- Saul of Tarsus (Acts 9:1-9; 22:16) would eventually be renamed Paul, the Apostle. After murdering countless Christians, Jesus placed scales on his eyes, taking away his vision. Paul was unable to physically see anything for three days, forced to accept what he'd done to Christians, accept that Jesus Christ was the Son of God and change his life to follow Jesus and preach the Gospel. His comfort came when Jesus removed the scales from his eyes. Thirteen of the twenty-seven books in the New Testament have traditionally been attributed to Paul being the author.

What if the grief and mourning someone is experiencing is not a result of their own sin, but a result of someone else's sin? In the parable of the Prodigal Son, the younger of two sons asks his father for his inheritance. After his father grants his request, the young son leaves home, money in hand and ready to live lavishly without anyone controlling him. The problem is, he's "prodigal" (i.e., wasteful and extravagant) and loses everything, eventually becoming destitute. He's forced to return home, ashamed with nothing to show for himself. He plans to beg his father to accept him back, hoping his dad will show mercy and allow him to stay and work as a servant. To the son's surprise, he's not met with condemnation by his father, but instead welcomed back with open arms and rejoicing! When the older son refuses to participate in the festivities, the father reminds the older son that one day he will inherit everything, and that they should still celebrate the return of the younger son because he was lost and is now found.

Christ promises to be the comforter of all who turn to Him, "Come to me, all who labor and are heavy laden, and I will give you rest. Take my yoke upon you, and learn from me; for I am gentle and lowly in heart, and you will find rest for your souls. For my yoke is easy, and my burden is light." (Matthew 11:28-30). When we experience suffering, we're immediately given one of the greatest gifts possible, a share of Christ's peace and love. That, my friends, is where the "blessing" lies in our most dark, devastating times of mourning.

Matthew 5:4 is true - Jesus really meets repentance with comfort, not reprimand. We never need to fear being exposed. At the end of Jesus' forty-day voluntary fast in the desert, angels were there to comfort him. Jesus was without sin, but the sins of the world were what the enemy and his demonic spirits used to torment Him those 40 days. Jesus Christ, the Son of God has experienced mourning of all kinds; he suffered the greatest death of all so that we would have God's comfort forever more. In times of mourning, we have hope. In the darkest seasons, we have the Light of God. In suffering, we have the ultimate comfort in The Comforter, Our Almighty Father. Amen and Amen!

DISCUSSION

1. Have there been seasons in your life as a mom of a special child when you felt like giving up? If so, how did you overcome those feelings?

2. Have you struggled with allowing yourself to mourn your child's challenges? Or do you feel like your time in mourning is still ongoing?

3. Do you go into "fix it" mode by taking control of difficult situations? If yes, why?

4. Have you experienced an unexplained peace in the middle of an extremely trying situation? Have you experienced a supernatural peace in the midst of turmoil and pain?

5. What is God pressing on your heart today?

DAY 1

ISAIAH 25:8

_____

_____

_____

_____

_____

_____

_____

_____

_____

_____

_____

_____

_____

_____

DAY 2

ISAIAH 40:1

_____

_____

_____

_____

_____

_____

_____

_____

_____

_____

_____

_____

_____

_____

DAY 3

PSALM 51:1-4

_____

_____

_____

_____

_____

_____

_____

_____

_____

_____

_____

_____

_____

_____

_____

DAY 4

LUKE 22:43

_____

_____

_____

_____

_____

_____

_____

_____

_____

_____

_____

_____

_____

_____

DAY 5

JAMES 5:16

_____

_____

_____

_____

_____

_____

_____

_____

_____

_____

_____

_____

_____

_____

Lesson 3

Blessed are the meek,
For they shall inherit the earth.

Matthew 5:5

If you were hiring someone for a leadership position, what characteristics would you look for in an applicant? If you consider the characteristics of the more successful leaders you've worked for, it's probably safe to say "meekness" wouldn't be a word you'd use to describe them. Open a Thesaurus, turn to the word "meek" and you'll see related words such as unaggressive, unassertive, cowering, ingenuous, or naïve. Meekness is often considered weakness; timidity and shyness aren't exactly character traits typically seen in a foreman or executive.

Often throughout the Bible, the word "meek" is translated from the Greek word "*praus.*"

Praus is defined as "strength brought under control"; some translations use the word "gentle." In other words, blessed are those whose strength is in their ability to let go of what doesn't matter; being gentle and humble in the face of persecution.

How often do you get offended? How easily are you upset by others? Have you been the victim of persecution from coworkers and/or family? I've yet to meet a special needs mom, or any mom for that matter, who hasn't been at the receiving end of bullying from an armchair quarterback. Unfortunately, we live in a secular world which means there are cruel people all around us.

Because we fiercely protect our babies, the enemy will use every weapon possible to tempt us to unleash anger on those who've hurt them. I promise you this—each of us WILL be baited by the enemy for a fight. Victory is guaranteed and the battle will end before it begins when GOD is the one defending us and our children.

THE CONDITION

In the book of Numbers 12:3, Moses was described as *"very humble, more than all men who were on the face of the earth."* The ASV and KJV translations say he was very "meek." How could his meekness be a blessing for Moses when being ridiculed?

READ Numbers 12:1-3

1. Who was complaining about Moses?

2. Why were they speak against him?

3. Who heard their conversation?

4. How was Moses described in verse 3?

Miriam and Aaron, Moses' older siblings, were feigning offense that Moses had married a foreign wife as the reason for their disdain; but most likely they were jealous of their younger brother. They thought it was ridiculous that any gift of Prophesy would skip over them and be given to their baby brother. Moses' superior authority from God brought out the envy and ugliness in these two. Moses could've thrown his being the chosen one right back in their face, but he didn't. And he wouldn't have. He was a gentle soul. God knew Moses would refrain from conflict; Moses knew he wouldn't win battles like that. Moses didn't respond to Miriam and Aaron, but God is about to.

READ Numbers 12:4-9

1. How would God typically communicate with His chosen prophets?

2. Moses was unique and God communicated differently with Him. Why is that? (verse 7)

3. How does God speak to Moses?

Experiencing a falling-out with family and/or friends is excruciatingly painful. When we are on the receiving end of unwanted, unacceptable, or unspeakable words and actions of others, <u>our</u> response is what matter most. There is no greater calm than the stillness that we experience by going straight to prayer for someone who's hurt us. It's only when we pause and pray that we are shielded by our Almighty Father. If in such circumstances we can hold fast to the gentleness and meekness of Moses, we will inherently forgive and let go.

I love The Message translation of Numbers 12:10-13,

Numbers 12:10-16 (MSG)

When the Cloud moved off from the Tent, oh! Miriam had turned leprous, her skin like snow. Aaron took one look at Miriam—a leper! He said to Moses, "Please, my master, please don't come down so hard on us for this foolish and thoughtless sin. Please don't make her like a stillborn baby coming out of its mother's womb with half its body decomposed."

And Moses prayed to God:

"Please, God, heal her, please heal her."

• What was Miriam's punishment?

• How did Aaron react?

• How did Moses react?

READ Numbers 12:14-16.

God bestows mercy on Aaron, but Miriam was going to have to suffer in quarantine for another 7 days. In verse 15, who else was impacted by her punishment? That's right, the entire camp!

Our *feelings* make us want to vindicate ourselves and our children, but God is the divine vindicator. God will only fight for us when we step out of His way, allowing God to be God. He chose us to be our children's moms because He knew *they* were going to show *us* what compassion, forgiveness, and immediate grace looks like. We honor our Savior Jesus Christ when we bestow the same compassion, forgiveness, and grace that He freely gave us on the Cross. We must be the hands and feet of Jesus to others, just like our special children are to us.

Biblical meekness requires supernatural strength—a quality that can only be produced by God in our lives.

READ 2 Timothy 2:22-26. Here Paul teaches what essential qualities of leadership are, and what leaders should avoid.

- Which of these qualities do you struggle with?

- Which of these qualities do you feel you have?

As moms, we must set the example we want our children to follow. Let's lead with purpose, leaving a legacy of gentleness and humility for generations to come.

THE RESULT

What does it mean that the meek will "inherit the earth"? God owns the earth—He created it! Therefore, He supplies all our needs so that we may safely dwell down here. Through Jesus, we become children of God when we accept Jesus Christ as our Lord and Savior. As children of God through His Son, we're automatically heirs to His Kingdom.

1. **God owns the earth** - *Psalms 24:1*

2. **And supplies all our needs** - *Philippians 4:19*

3. **By obedience to Jesus, we become children of God** - *Hebrews 5:9*

4. **As children of God, we're heirs in the Kingdom of Christ** - *Ephesians 5:5* (Kingdom <u>NOW</u> through <u>GRACE</u>)

5. **Therefore our place in Heaven is reserved** *–1 Peter 1:4-5* (our Father's house)

> "SEEK THE LORD, ALL YOU HUMBLE OF THE LAND, YOU WHO DO WHAT HE COMMANDS. SEEK RIGHTEOUSNESS, SEEK HUMILITY; PERHAPS YOU WILL BE SHELTERED ON THE DAY OF THE LORD'S ANGER." (ZEPHANIAH 2:3 NIV)

If we are empty of God and His Word, we will fill our lives with pride, vanity, control, sin, and resentment. This leads to idolatry, which leads to immorality, which leads to darkness and disaster. If we aren't filled with God, especially in times of despair and darkness, then we're left hopeless. If we don't repent of our sins, we will never be free. The weight of the chains wrapped in sin will never be broken, therefore holding us hostage in a battle we'll never win. If we allow our feelings to be our compass, we will find ourselves in the middle of a war with only ourselves to blame. That war will destroy generations to come.

I'm so grateful that God reveals His love for us every week. What we once saw as a disability, God is revealing to be His ability. DISABILITY = HIS ABILITY. Amen and Amen!!!

DISCUSSION

1. Do you struggle with being easily offended?

2. How do you handle situations when someone has said hurtful things to you or your children?

3. Does this lesson make you want to activate the "pause button" more than you normally would?

4. When offended or under attack, do you typically respond or react to the situation?

5. What is the Lord saying to you through this lesson?

DAY 1

2 PETER 3:10-12

_____

_____

_____

_____

_____

_____

_____

_____

_____

_____

_____

_____

_____

_____

DAY 2

ZEPHANIAH 2:3

_____

_____

_____

_____

_____

_____

_____

_____

_____

_____

_____

_____

_____

DAY 3

GALATIANS 5:23-26

_____

_____

_____

_____

_____

_____

_____

_____

_____

_____

_____

_____

_____

_____

_____

_____

DAY 4

MATTHEW 5:38-42

_____

_____

_____

_____

_____

_____

_____

_____

_____

_____

_____

_____

_____

_____

DAY 5

MATTHEW 5: 43-48

_____

_____

_____

_____

_____

_____

_____

_____

_____

_____

_____

_____

_____

_____

_____

Lesson 4

"Blessed are those who hunger and thirst for righteousness, for they will be filled."

Matthew 5:6

The most fundamental human experience is our need to eat and drink. God designed us to require food and water in order to survive. Without food and water, we will die. Can we survive without cars, social media, cell phones, Netflix, devices, lip balm, Starbucks, or yoga? Yes, of course we can, we'd just rather not. What about the proverbial "bucket list"? We all have one—a list of people we'd love to meet, places we dream of vacationing, and luxurious things we'd love to indulge in. What is it about the lure, the temptation of what we don't have that's so attractive?

If we asked God to show us what our bucket lists look like through spiritual eyes, He'd reveal so much more than vacations to white sand beaches and spending the afternoon cooking with Oprah Winfrey in her kitchen. Through spiritual eyes, you'll see art imitating life. The only problem is the "masterpiece" staring back at you isn't an authentic *master*piece. What's revealed is a dark, bleak, black and white sketch of the Garden of Eden. Your spiritual eyes will be instantly drawn to the Tree of Life that's prominently placed front and center; the only burst of color shining brightly is the forbidden fruit.

The condition of those who are blessed in the scriptures each week is very important; this week the condition isn't as obvious. Many people assume the condition of *those who hunger and thirst for righteousness* is the righteousness itself. What is righteousness?

Merriam-Webster Dictionary defines "righteousness"-

1. Acting in accord with divine or moral law; free from guilt or sin

2. Morally right or justifiable

Those definitions might give you a better idea of what righteousness means, but what does it mean to live righteously in accordance with the Beatitude Jesus is teaching in Matthew 5:6?

Scripture tells us over and over again that righteousness is the state of moral perfection required by God to enter Heaven.

The Bible clearly states that human beings <u>cannot achieve righteousness through their own efforts</u>. We, therefore *"fall short of God's glory" (Romans 3:23)*. As believers in Jesus Christ, we're given the gift of being able to live a life in alignment with God. Through our faith in Christ, the righteousness of God is given to us. (This is called "imputed" righteousness. To impute something is to ascribe or attribute something to someone.) When we hunger and thirst for righteousness, our desires change. Without a HUNGER for God, we will have very little desire for righteousness.

THE CONDITION

How often do you crave Chick-Fil-A on Sundays but don't eat there the rest of the week? All too often we want what *we* want, when *we* want it, at *our* convenience.

In Luke 14, Jesus is eating at the home of another Pharisee. They were breaking bread together on this Sabbath day when Jesus noticed another guest who suffered from "dropsy." Jesus, knowing the guests would be appalled at His "working" on the Sabbath, took hold of this man and removed many pounds/gallons of fluid from his body in a few seconds. As He always does, Jesus takes this opportunity to speak into the lives of all who were there.

READ Luke 14:16-20

1. What was the event being held?

2. Of those invited, who attended?

3. What were the reasons the guests gave for not coming? List them below.

   - Excuse 1: _____

   - Excuse 2: _____

   - Excuse 3: _____

This sounds like an incredible party! The host has put forth so much love and effort into preparing such an event and is left with no guests. They were all busy doing what they wanted to do. Clearly the guests knew about the party and had accepted the invitation to come. Breaks the heart of the host, but he comes up with a better plan.

READ Luke 14:21-24

1. Who was the slave instructed to invite?

2. According to verse 22, was the house filled yet?

3. What does the host say about those he'd originally invited?

Here's Jesus point: just because the meal was prepared and the host invited guests, there was no guarantee the guests were going to show up and want to eat any of it. In this parable, God is the host; eternal life is the party; but not everyone who's invited is interested in coming. They're busy doing *what they* want, going *where they* want, *when they* want. Clearly, they're not hungry or thirsty for anything God has to offer. Righteousness will <u>never</u> be theirs. Heaven will <u>not</u> be an option for them. To hunger and thirst is to seek God with every fiber of your being. Rejoice in your condition of starvation, your unrelenting need for Him.

WRITE Matthew 6:33 in the space below.

_____

_____

_____

_____

_____

THE RESULT

Those who hunger and thirst for righteousness are the only ones perfectly positioned to be filled. Some translations say, *"For they will be satisfied."* We know that God cannot fill what is full; this is a beautiful common thread that God continues to reveal each week. Jesus is telling us over and over again that we must remain empty, cling to that emptiness, and never fill ourselves with anything other than HIM. The moment we're away from God, the enemy slithers in, ready to kill, steal, and destroy. And he wastes no time. It's only 3 chapters into the Bible where the enemy makes his debut.

READ Genesis 3:1-4

1. The serpent is described as the most _____ of all the animals.

2. Who was the serpent quoting in his question to Eve in verse 1?

3. How did Eve respond to the serpent?

READ Genesis 3:5-7

1. In verse 5, who did the serpent say would be like God as a result of eating the forbidden fruit?

2. List the three ways Eve sees the fruit of the tree in verse 6.

   • _____ for food,

   • _____ to look at, and

   • _____ for obtaining _____.

Eve wasn't tempted because she was hungry for the fruit on the Tree of Life; God's provision of food and drink was endless in the Garden of Eden. In fact, they'd never experienced hunger pains, nor pain at all for that matter. What the enemy knew that Adam and Eve didn't was that God created them with free will. Temptation was the bait on the end of the enemy's line and Eve fell for it, taking Adam down with her as they fell from grace.

READ Genesis 3:8-13

1. Who were Adam and Eve hiding from?

2. Who did God call out to?

3. Why did they hide?

4. In verse 12, who did Adam blame?

5. Who did Eve blame?

READ Genesis 3:14-16

God immediately unleashed His wrath, handing down punishments one at a time. The enemy was cursed, animosity put in place between the serpent and Eve and all their offspring. Eve was next on the chopping block, being cursed with bearing children and pain in doing so. As hard as that punishment would be, it's nothing compared to her final punishment in the end of verse 16.

"Your desire will be for your husband,
and he will rule over you."

Genesis 3:16 (NASB)

From that point on, Eve would desire Adam above God. She would have to desire God by *choice*, not by *nature*. Adam would rule over her, not God. She would have to hunger and thirst for God who would no longer have a place in her life without an invitation. These devastating repercussions were in place until our Savior, Jesus Christ, paid the ultimate price upon the cross. When we place our faith in Christ, God ascribes the perfect righteousness of Christ to our account so that we become perfect in His sight. *"For our sake he made him to be sin who knew no sin, so that in him we might become the righteousness of God" (2 Corinthians 5:21).*

The enemy will slither in uninvited, in the dark, as quietly as possible to remain undetected. He is crafty, subtle, hypocritical, and has trained his army well. God asked Eve a question that can't be overlooked, "Who told you that?" When we hunger and thirst for God and His presence in our lives, we will be able to immediately recognize the wrong voice when it speaks to us. Perhaps you've heard statements from others and/or suffered from thoughts of your own, such as:

- Your child won't ever be able to _____.

- Your child can't _____.

- You'll never be able to _____ as a family.

- Your child is _____.

- I'm such a _____ as a mom.

- It's my fault my child is like this.

- It's never going to get better.

- Other:

Who said those things to you? Was it a doctor and/or specialist who told you what your child's limitations would be? Has an educator told you how smart your child is (or isn't)? Your own thoughts may sound like your voice, but do not be fooled like Eve was in the Garden that day. WHO told her that the fruit was good to eat? She didn't convince herself, did she?

The ultimate healer, divine specialist, miracle making and life changing God Almighty is the ONLY voice that matters. God's word spoken over our lives and the lives of our children is thunderous. We will know its God we're hearing, distinct and crystal clear as we crave filling ourselves with all of HIM. We are blessed because we hunger and thirst to receive Him! I pray that we are never satisfied with anything—limitations, diagnosis, parameters, WebMD, opinions of others, lies from our past.

We'll never find our Kingdom Purpose in this journey if we're too busy focusing on what the enemy distracts us with—what we don't have. Hunger and thirst come from a place of emptiness. We're four weeks into being empty and you're not only surviving, you're *thriving* in the name of Jesus! Hallelujah!

DISCUSSION

1. How has God's word today impacted you regarding the limitations of your child that the world has placed upon them?

2. How has God's word today impacted you regarding the lies you've believed about yourself as a parent?

3. How has God's word today impacted you regarding your self-identity, insecurity, and guilt? Who told you that?

4. Do you struggle with a desperate need for things that you don't have? Has anything about your desire changed today?

5. Are you hungry for God? Are you thirsting for His presence in your life? If not, what are you seeking the most in this present season?

DAY 1

LUKE 14:12-14

_____

_____

_____

_____

_____

_____

_____

_____

_____

_____

_____

_____

_____

DAY 2

LUKE 6:21

_____

_____

_____

_____

_____

_____

_____

_____

_____

_____

_____

_____

_____

DAY 3

PSALM 42:1-2

_____

_____

_____

_____

_____

_____

_____

_____

_____

_____

_____

_____

_____

_____

_____

DAY 4

ISAIAH 55:1-2

_____

_____

_____

_____

_____

_____

_____

_____

_____

_____

_____

_____

_____

_____

DAY 5

HEBREWS 13:12

_____

_____

_____

_____

_____

_____

_____

_____

_____

_____

_____

_____

_____

_____

Lesson 5

Blessed are the merciful,
for they shall receive mercy.

Matthew 5:7

The first three beatitudes in Matthew 5:3-5 shared a common theme that pressed upon us the absolute need to be empty: poverty of spirit (verse 3), grieving sin—one's own sin or the sin of a loved one leads to mourning and produces repentance (verse 4), and gently (meekly) moving aside so that God can fight the battles of cruel and hurtful judgement (verse 5). Understanding the importance of our emptiness, being void of self, left us hungry and thirsty for Christ, who was then able fill our emptiness with His righteousness (verse 6).

How does righteousness abound in the hearts of the hungry? How do we, the hungry disciples of Jesus, begin to see and experience the changes God is making within our spirit? Jesus describes the heart change in the life of a Christian who is starving for righteous living three ways—in mercy (verse 7), in purity (verse 8), and in peacemaking (verse 9).

THE CONDITION

What is mercy? What's your definition of a merciful person? Does a particular friend or family member come to mind whom you feel is merciful? Do you struggle with showing mercy toward others? If you're not sure, it's okay—we'll have a clear understanding of the characteristics God sees in a "merciful" person by the end of this lesson.

Merriam-Webster definition of *Merciful*

1. Treating people with kindness and forgiveness

2. Not cruel or harsh

3. Having or showing mercy

4. Giving relief from suffering

Based on the definitions above, it's clear that mercy is given and/or received from one person to another. As a mom of two special needs kids, I often struggle with when to discipline and when to be tenderly merciful, carefully approaching both sides of blurred lines. Because our children are unlike "typical" kids their age, the standards to which we hold them accountable are different. My daughter is much higher functioning than my son and can process the reason we have rules and the dangerous repercussions in breaking them, both at home and at school.

My son on the other hand understands what "no" means and knows when he's doing something that's not allowed. He proves that when he sneaks our cell phones and runs up to his room, locking it behind him. When it comes to creating a standard of discipline for our children who are different, what matters most is the grace and love that drives us. The answer is simple: we remind ourselves that we are not without sin, yet have been forgiven.

READ Luke 6:36-38 then fill in the blanks below.

Do not _____ and you will not be _____.

Do not _____ and you will not be _____.

_____ and you will be _____.

_____ and it will be _____ to you.

Nothing moves us to forgive others like the revelation that God has forgiven *our* sins. Mercy toward others begins in our hearts when we experience His forgiveness for ourselves. There is nothing that proves more convincingly that we have been forgiven than when our readiness to forgive is innate and *without* bias. Being merciful and kind is evidence that God has given us His Spirit. When we have the Holy Spirit alive inside our hearts, we begin to see others as God sees them.

READ Matthew 25:34-36.

1. What were the 6 things Jesus needed from others?

2. Were His needs met?

3. Who does Jesus say helped Him?

Continue READING Matthew 25:38-40.

4. How did the people respond to Jesus in verses 38 and 39?

5. What is Jesus' response in verse 40? WRITE verse 40 in the space below.

_____

_____

_____

_____

_____

Now, go back to the first question regarding Matthew 25:34-36 and circle each need in your answers that you've met for your own special children. If you didn't circle the last one about Jesus being in prison, let me ask you to take a minute and consider something you may have never considered before—is your child's disability or additional needs somewhat of a prison for them?

Pray and ask the Holy Spirit to show you who it is you are serving when you are taking care of your children. The "least of these" are anyone who cannot help themselves. If you want further confirmation, re-read your handwritten words of Matthew 25:40.

If you'd never considered your beautifully "special" children to be living images of Jesus, I pray that you now know they *are*. THIS changed everything for me in my journey as a mom of two special needs children! It's still a difficult road ahead and not always fun, but my understanding of my Kingdom Purpose has changed everything! I pray it changes your perspective as well.

Most likely Jesus spoke in Aramaic, and the idea behind His statement about mercy comes from the Old Testament (Hebrew) usage and teaching. The word Jesus would have used is the Hebrew and Aramaic "*chesed.*" Take a look at William Barclay's *Daily Study Bible* commentary on Matthew regarding this word:

> It does not mean only to sympathize with a person in the popular sense of the term; it does not mean simply to feel sorry for some in trouble. *Chesedh* [sic], *mercy,* means the ability to get right inside the other person›s skin until we can see things with his eyes, think things with his mind, and feel things with his feelings. Clearly this is much more than an emotional wave of pity; clearly this demands a quite deliberate effort of the mind and of the will. It denotes a sympathy which is not given, as it were, from outside, but which comes from a deliberate identification with the other person, until we see things as he sees them, and feel things as he feels them. This is *sympathy* in the literal sense of the word *Sympathy* means *experiencing things together with the other person,* literally going through what he is going through. (p. 103)

Our precious children have created a sympathetic heart in us that we might not have had otherwise! God doesn't want us to limit our rendering of love, compassion, and empathy to the confines of our home; He has chosen us to go out and be the living, breathing hands and feet of Jesus. With this calling on our lives, our Kingdom Purpose will draw us into ministry and stir our hearts to be God's boots on the ground.

THE RESULT

People offering mercy to others results in God's divine, tender mercy in return. Matthew 6:14 is a beautiful example this, *"For if you forgive men their trespasses, your heavenly Father will also forgive you."* The mercy Jesus teaches is not humanly derived. This happens, not because we can earn mercy by generosity or forgiving of others, but because <u>we cannot receive the mercy and forgiveness of GOD unless we repent</u>. We cannot claim to have repented of *our sins* if we are unmerciful towards the sins *of others*.

It's impossible for Jesus to change from what He is, but we can and *must* change to be like Him.

The world we live in is suffering from a lack of mercy on practically every level. We can't watch the evening news without being bombarded with harsh opinions; the media's play on words and semantics victoriously causing strife. The epidemic of HATE is spreading like wildfire and the enemy's armies, infected with the serpent's venom, are working overtime.

READ Ephesians 6:12

1. Who does the Apostle Paul tell us we're NOT wrestling with?

2. Who ARE we actually being attacked by?

The barbarian mindset that operates in *FEAR* is nothing new. In the Old Testament world, a barbarian's strength was measured by their ability to control and dominate with fear. To this day, the purpose behind every single violent protest, act of terrorism, and false pretenses that glamorize vanity is this: to inflict fear in all of us.

Fear and/or insecurity give the enemy an open door to wreak havoc over and over again. His entrance quickly weaves a stronghold over our thoughts, lives and our homes. The darkness that he brings begins constantly filling us with FEAR of the unknown and fear that our children won't be okay without us as their primary caretakers. Satan has done everything possible to convince you, me, and thousands of other moms around the world that our fragile children will only be "safe" while they're under <u>our</u> care. How many hours of sleep have you lost thinking, "If and when I die, what will happen to my baby? WHO will take care of my child?"

Have you ever fell victim to the biggest, most catastrophic lie the enemy tells? Here it is:

"I must outlive my child." Only the devil could've tricked you into praying that you outlive your children. Thoughts like this are NOT of God.

> *And do not be conformed to this world, but be transformed by the renewing of your mind, that you may prove what is* that good and acceptable and perfect will of God.
>
> *Romans 12:2 (NKJV)*

God is preparing us - the spiritually poor, sorrowful and repentant for our own sin, meek and free from defensiveness, hungry and thirsty for righteousness, empathetic, and merciful—for a paradigm shift. A paradigm is "an example that serves as a pattern or model." A paradigm shift is significant and can change the way society perceives things. A *spiritual paradigm shift* was desperately needed in our lives as moms of special needs children. Week after week, our perspectives have changed; our spiritual eyes are being opened, revealing God's Kingdom Perspective in our Kingdom Purpose journey.

God desperately wants to shift our perception of the world around us— beginning with our immediate circle. As we grow, He begins helping us see others as God sees them and love them as He loves them. Our prayers inherently evolve without realizing it when God takes up residence inside our spirits.

Prepare yourselves for the next couple weeks as God reveals His power working within you. His Kingdom Perspective has already begun shifting your perspective. With this new Kingdom mindset, your heart will be supernaturally transformed to a Heart for the Kingdom. Those with a Kingdom Heart are the merciful, the pure, and the peacemakers.

My dear friends, Dr. Tracey Sharpe and his wife Linda wrote a book called *Reaching People and Touching Lives Around the World*. Together they've ministered internationally, reaching out to lost souls as missionaries and have a combined total of over 30 years in ministry. Jesus taught the Sermon on the Mount to His disciples so that they would be spiritually transformed from their way of thinking to God's way of thinking. Meditate on the passages below that I took from their book; ask the Holy Spirit to reveal this week what God is saying to you.

A spiritual paradigm shift that moves believers from one way of thinking (locally) to another (globally) is necessary for change to take place in the church. This can come about only through a transformation of the minds and hearts of believers. As we grow in Christ, we will stagnate at one level of spiritual development and never mature into the people God intended us to be unless we are willing to embrace new paradigms. But God will help us and create situations that allow our paradigms to shift in order to bring us out of the past and the future and into the "right now." Faith is *now*, and we must believe that whatever we ask for in prayer will happen *now*.

(p.38, Reaching People and Touching Lives Around the World)

DISCUSSION

1. Can you remember a moment in your life where you were shown undeserved mercy by a friend, family member, or stranger?

2. Have you been hurt by someone else's lack of forgiveness or harsh judgement toward you?

3. Do you harbor anger toward someone that you feel God is asking you to forgive?

4. Where do you feel the Holy Spirit supernaturally shifting your perspective in regard to your child's disability?

5. What do you feel God is saying to you in this lesson?

DAY 1

JOHN 15:16

_____

_____

_____

_____

_____

_____

_____

_____

_____

_____

_____

_____

_____

DAY 2

MATTHEW 9:13

_____

_____

_____

_____

_____

_____

_____

_____

_____

_____

_____

_____

_____

_____

DAY 3

COLOSSIANS 3:12-14

_____

_____

_____

_____

_____

_____

_____

_____

_____

_____

_____

_____

_____

_____

DAY 4

2 SAMUEL 22:24-25

_____

_____

_____

_____

_____

_____

_____

_____

_____

_____

_____

_____

_____

_____

DAY 5

EPHESIANS 4:22 & 6:4

_____

_____

_____

_____

_____

_____

_____

_____

_____

_____

_____

_____

_____

Lesson 6

Blessed are the pure in heart,
for they will see God.

Matthew 5:8

Last week we learned that we're only able to be merciful to others because God has shown us mercy by forgiving our sins. This week will focus on a very personal area of ourselves—our hearts. As women, we're not typically thought of as being uncomfortable when talking about our feelings, desires, and affections but being pure of heart goes way beyond emotions. Once again, the spiritual paradigm shift we learned about last week plays a major role in our becoming *pure in heart.*

Remember, a *paradigm* is "an example that serves as a pattern or model." A paradigm shift is significant and changes the way society perceives things. A *spiritual paradigm shift* was desperately needed in our lives as moms of special needs children. Week after week, our perspectives have changed; our spiritual eyes are being opened, revealing God's Kingdom Perspective in our Kingdom Purpose journey.

Purity of heart is an intentional, conscious exertion to be pure in thought *and* action. This is a team effort with shared responsibility between the one who is pure in heart and God. We know that our sins are washed clean when God has forgiven them, but this is different. The *pure in heart* are those who seek to remain free of every form of sin and doing so with all their being.

THE CONDITION

The condition of being pure in heart is dependent on both the inward and outward state of being. God sees our hearts and minds as one in the same; doing good works with deceptive motives at the core is more common than you think. Our innermost thoughts and intentions are silent to everyone except our omniscient Father. His awareness of our objectives, goals, dreams, and schemes is infinite. Life on earth ends when a heart stops beating, but the <u>secrecy</u> of our innermost thoughts and feelings is the determining factor regarding our eternal of life.

WRITE Proverbs 4:23 in the space below.

_____

_____

_____

_____

_____

Merriam-Webster dictionary defines "pure"

1. Not mixed with anything else

2. Clean and not harmful in any way

3. Having a smooth and clear sound that is not mixed with any other sound

The Greek word for "pure" is *katharos,* as used in Matthew 5:8, which describes a heart that is pure in motive and exhibits single mindedness, undivided devotion and spiritual integrity.

READ Psalm 24:3-4

1. In verse 3, David asks God, *"who will ascend the hill of the Lord and stand in His Holy place?"* What is the answer in verse 4?

The answer follows in verse 4, the one *"who has clean hands and a pure heart"*, describes a person who is the same both in public and in private. We might assume we are good people because we're nice to everyone but God's standards are at a much higher level than niceties. In order to be pure in heart, we need to step out of ourselves and evaluate who we truly are when no one is around but God.

READ 1 Samuel 16:7

1. What does man look at in determining someone's heart?

2. What does the Lord look at instead?

*<u>WARNING</u>! The following questions are uncomfortable but don't worry, you don't have to answer any of them out loud. This exercise is NOT to condemn, but rather to bring awareness of where your heart is. Many of us are unknowingly housing hearts that are not exactly pure.

A. Do you wish God would hurry up and answer your prayers but never take time to love, talk to, and build a relationship with Him out of *want* instead of *need*?

B. Do you curse when your kids aren't around but clean up your language when they're with you? Or do you curse all the time no matter who's around?

C. Do you ignore the elderly person pushing an empty shopping cart to the cart return because they're across the parking lot and you're in a hurry?

D. Do you say you'll pray for someone, but you don't?

E. Do you put more effort into matters of personal *gain* (such as social status, money, possessions) but avoid tithing because you feel you're *losing* monetarily?

F. Do you wish your husband were more like his good looking, successful friend(s)?

If any of these questions resonated with you then you have a heart condition—an impurity of heart condition. If your actions appear to be true, yet the motives behind them are impure, you need to realize your need for God is great. If your thoughts and motives are self-centered, it will be impossible for you to live a God-centered life. To some, the example above about the elderly person may sound less like impurity of heart and more like happenstance, but don't let the enemy try to confuse you. There is a big difference between irony and impurity. We can't risk committing "small" offenses because we don't serve a small God. Our lives must be lived with pure hearts.

THE RESULT

The result of having a pure heart is what's so majestic about this beatitude—we will see God. When we are living in alignment with the Lord - from the inside out - He allows us to see Him in everything. We will see Him in scripture, in nature, at church, in strangers, in our homes and in ourselves! The Greek word *katharos* gives us our English word "catharsis" which is used to describe a cleansing of one's mind or emotions. There is nothing more cathartic than being in the presence of God.

Our spiritual paradigm shifts begin outwardly when we're merciful to others without hesitation. As God sees that we see Jesus in others, He blesses us with more than just His mercy cleansing our sins, He gives us new hearts. It's with this new heart that our mindset continues to shift and grow our perspective at home and in the world around us.

"³⁹ then I will give them one heart and one way, that they may fear Me forever, for the good of them and their children after them."

Jeremiah 32:39 (NKJV)

Let's compare God's word below to each of the uncomfortable questions we discussed earlier in the lesson:

A. *Psalm* 9:10

B. Matthew 12:33-34

C. Hebrews 13:2

D. Galatians 1:10

E. Matthew 19:21

F. Matthew *5:27-28*

Only the pure are capable of seeing God. God refuses to look upon those living in sin and covered by their iniquities. The reason why selfish prayers aren't answered and Atheists still exist is because they can't see His purity. God doesn't hear their prayers and won't allow them to see Him. We must pray for everyone who loves God, seeks Him, but most of all we must pray for those who don't. How can we call ourselves Christians if we're only praying for the people we love when it's convenient? There's nothing merciful in withholding prayer for lost souls.

Letting go and letting God does not mean doing what's easiest with the least amount of effort. The hardest work we'll ever do is giving God complete control and surrendering to His will. This requires a pure heart that is patient and trusting that He is faithful regardless of the outcome.

God is active and visible all around us when we keep sin out of our lives. This is an ongoing, daily battle that is not always easy to fight, but the victory is the Kingdom of Heaven now through GRACE, and the hereafter through GLORY. Give everything God takes without hesitation, and take everything

God gives with complete humility and thanksgiving to Him. Be vigilant in your obedience and remain hungry and thirsty for righteousness. The Lord will satisfy and fill you with endless mercy and a pure heart.

2 Set your minds on things above, not on earthly things. 3 For you died, and your life is now hidden with Christ in God. 4 When Christ, who is your life, appears, then you also will appear with him in glory.

Colossians 3:2-4 (NIV)

DISCUSSION

1. Do you struggle with transparency?

2. Does it matter that God sees you AND your innermost thoughts and desires?

3. Do you believe Jesus is who He says He is?

4. As of this very moment, would you say you're pure in heart?

5. If not, what changes do you need to make in your life and thoughts to become pure in heart according to God?

DAY 1

JAMES 1 (READ the whole chapter, only write the verses that deeply resonate with you.)

_____

_____

_____

_____

_____

_____

_____

_____

_____

_____

_____

_____

DAY 2

JAMES 2 (READ the whole chapter, only write the verses that speak boldly to you.)

_____

_____

_____

_____

_____

_____

_____

_____

_____

_____

_____

_____

_____

_____

DAY 3

JAMES 3 (READ the whole chapter, only write the verses that you feel are areas you need to work on.)

_____

_____

_____

_____

_____

_____

_____

_____

_____

_____

_____

_____

DAY 4

JAMES 4 (READ the whole chapter, only write the verses that stir your spirit.)

_____

_____

_____

_____

_____

_____

_____

_____

_____

_____

_____

_____

_____

DAY 5

JAMES 5 (READ the whole chapter, only write the verses that stir your spirit.)

_____

_____

_____

_____

_____

_____

_____

_____

_____

_____

_____

_____

_____

_____

Lesson 7

Blessed are the peacemakers,
For they shall be called children of God.

Matthew 5:9

We have spent the last 6 weeks in pursuit of a deeper understanding of the Beatitudes Jesus taught in the Sermon on the Mount (Matthew 5) and the Sermon on the Plains (Luke 6). God has revealed significant, personal words for each of us throughout this study and the breakthroughs we've had are not by coincidence. What we will see today is the intentional, divine poetry Jesus delivered that unify the blessings of the merciful (verse 7), the pure in heart (verse 8), and the peacemakers (verse 9).

In week 5, we began to learn how righteousness can abound in the hearts *of those who hunger and thirst for righteousness (Matthew 5:6)*. Our spiritual paradigm shift began with becoming merciful, moving us to forgive others as God has forgiven us. We learned that, unless we've repented of our own sins, we will be unmerciful and unforgiving towards the sins of others. Last week (week 6) continued the shifting of a merciful spirit by becoming the same inwardly and outwardly, housing a heart that is pure. A person who has a pure heart seeks to remain free of every form of sin and does so with all their being. A merciful, pure-hearted person's rebirth is made complete by the <u>peace</u> that resides within them.

Let's look closely at the word "peacemaker". This compound word is comprised of two common words: "peace" and "maker".

"PEACE"

- *Shalom* is the Greek word for peace.

- In Hebrew, the word shalom signifies a sense of well-being and harmony both within and without - completeness, wholeness, peace, health, welfare, safety, soundness, tranquility, prosperity, fullness, rest, harmony; the absence of agitation or discord, a state of calm without anxiety or stress (into which Satan cannot enter).

- *Shalom* is used as a "hello" or "goodbye" among Jewish people. When a Jewish person says "Shalom" they're wishing on another the full presence, peace, and prosperity of all the blessedness of God. A clear example of this is found in the 6th chapter of the Book of Numbers.

READ Numbers 6:24-26 and WRITE it in the space below.

_____

_____

_____

_____

_____

_____

_____

_____

"MAKER"

- The word *make* in the term "peacemakers" comes from the Greek verb that means "to do" or "to make". It requires action and initiative.

- Peace must be made because it never happens by accident.

- By taking the initiative, peacemakers actively pursue peace.

The same word used in this Beatitude, peacemakers, is applied by the apostle Paul to what God has done through Christ so that we could be at peace with God. Through Christ God was pleased ". . . *to reconcile everything to Himself by making peace through the blood of His cross" (Col. 1:20)*. Paul also informed us that Jesus ". . . *might create in Himself one new man from the two, resulting in peace" (Eph. 2:15)*.

THE CONDITION

Peacemakers are those who

1. Pursue more than the absence of conflict

2. Don't avoid strife (like Jesus, peacemaking will sometimes create strife)

3. Aren't merely seeking to appease the warring parties

4. Aren't trying to accommodate everyone

Peacemakers choose to honor God, not win an argument. Peacemakers have harmonious relationships and have the supernatural ability, through the Holy Spirit, to embrace differences. Does that mean peacemakers go with the flow? No, they work at it as stated in the NLT of Matthew 5:9, *"God blesses those who work for peace."* William Barclay translates this verse: "They are people who produce right relationships in every sphere of life."

Once again, we're reminded of the spiritual paradigm shift God is inviting us to be a part of. The pattern of this world continues to be modeled by the Barbarian mindset established long ago in the Old Testament times. Barbarians operate in FEAR and work to create division through conflict and controversy. God's *children* have, and will always be, the few and far between—those who pattern their lives according to the model set forth by Jesus Christ. Peacemakers take the initiative and spring into <u>action</u> in hopes of resolving conflict.

READ Matthew 5:23-24.

1. Does Jesus say it's best to go directly to God in prayer to ask Him how you should handle a disagreement you're having with a friend or loved one?

2. Does Jesus suggest waiting for God to answer you before reaching out to the one you're in a disagreement with?

3. In verse 24, what does Jesus say to do first? What does He say to do next?

READ Matthew 18:15 and fill in the blanks.

15 *"Moreover if your brother _____ against you, go and tell _____ his fault between you and him _____. If he _____ you, you have _____ your brother."*

Does anyone come to mind for you, personally, whom you've battled in an ongoing conflict or harbor unforgiveness toward? Is there someone who refuses to forgive you? Is there someone whose forgiveness you've not sought out, but feel the need to repent and ask them to forgive you now? Write their name(s) in the space below. I pray that you will reach out to them, regardless of the circumstances. If doing so feels overwhelming or impossible, ask God to give you the words and the courage.

In his first letter to the Thessalonians, the Apostle Paul wrote to the members of the new church in Thessalonica to address problems they were facing.

The church of Thessalonica was made up of new Christians who had just come to Christ under Paul's ministry. Paul had to leave town in order to remain safe and continue to spread the Gospel because the pagans of Thessalonica were severely persecuting Christians at this time. Without Paul's presence, the members of this church were at high risk of falling away from the Lord. There were struggles among the new Christians, especially when it came to the members who wanted to be in charge. The power struggle was real, and so was the struggle among some to remain morally righteous. Paul's final prayer in his letter to the members speaks directly to the need for them to remain peacemakers, among themselves, and everyone they encountered in order to honor their calling and receive salvation.

READ 1 Thessalonians 5:15-23, then SUMMARIZE it in your own words below.

_____

_____

_____

_____

_____

_____

In today's world, the tendency in relationships, ranging from families to politics, is to ignore conflict or cover it up by using force, threats, or intimidation. The internet and tabloids are filled with rumors and gossip which go against BOTH the ability to be pure in heart or a peacemaker. God sees the hearts and minds of the people in all sides of conflict—those who devise the attacks and those who actively work to establish truth.

His *children* seek HIM when adversity comes their way and they will go to work, building bridges for their adversary to safely cross regardless of the conflict. In God's kingdom, it is a blessing when people who are divided are brought together. It's practically impossible to resolve conflict and restore broken relationships unless there is a peacemaker among them.

James 1:19-21 (NASB)

"¹⁹ *This* you know, my beloved brethren. But everyone must be quick to hear, slow to speak *and* slow to anger; ²⁰ *for the anger of man does not achieve the righteousness of God.* ²¹ *Therefore, putting aside all filthiness and all* that remains of wickedness, in humility receive the word implanted, which is able to save your souls."

The level of pain and heartbreak suffered at the hands of others may vary, but the discomfort and/or disdain when praying for our enemies is the same— gut-wrenching. Living with hate and abhorrence in our hearts immediately brings us out of alignment with God. Remember, God sees our hearts and minds as one in the same, making it impossible to hide thoughts of antipathy, hostility, jealousy, and malice. Just because you're not actively trying to ruin someone's life doesn't make it less of a risk to your salvation.

READ Hebrews 12:15-17.

1. Does Paul emphasize the importance of watching out solely for yourself or to be in union as a community and watch out for each other as well?

2. Do you have a solid, healthy faith-based circle of friends who will hold you accountable if you begin to veer off track and risk receiving God's grace? If so, do you accept their wisdom easily?

Forgiveness is an action. It's not a feeling. If your pain or resentment holds you back from forgiving someone, you're giving them power and time in your life. That being said, you can begin *acting* on the forgiveness without the discomfort of *feeling it*.

How are we supposed to pray for those who persecute us? The answer is in the middle of the Sermon on the Mount and will most likely surprise you. It's a prayer we pray every single day:

Matthew 6:8-13, The Lord's Prayer. What is most important when praying for your enemies? That you pray for them BY NAME. Simply add their name to verse 9, "Our Father who is in Heaven, _____ and *I* hallow Your name…" and finish the rest of the Lord's prayer as you normally would. This is where the spiritual paradigm shift begins in our adversaries' hearts. Begin right now, praying OUT LOUD with their name included.

> Our Father in heaven, _____ and I Hallow Your name. Your kingdom come. Your will be done on earth as it is in heaven. Give us this day our daily bread. And forgive us our trespasses, As we forgive those who trespass against us. And do not lead us into temptation, but deliver us from the evil one. For Yours is the kingdom and the power and the glory forever. Amen.

As a result of praying for your adversary, God will begin working in and around you (and the one you're praying for) in ways He couldn't otherwise!

- *God will hear the prayers* you lift up as ask that your enemy would hallow God's name.

- *God will hear your prayer* that God's Kingdom would come into the heart of your enemy.

- *God will hear your prayers* that He gives your enemy their daily bread and forgiveness, just as He's forgiven YOU.

- *God will hear your prayer* that your enemy's bondage of temptation from Satan will deliver them back into the hands of their Jehovah-shalom (the Lord send Peace).

- *God will reign* blessings down on you for your obedience and mercy. (He is SOVE<u>REIGN</u>)

- *He will give you* a pure heart and the chains withholding your forgiveness will be broken.

Matthew 6:14-15 are preceded by the Lord's prayer appropriately when praying for those who have hurt us deeply. It's as if Jesus knew that this would be a major breakthrough for you, therefore He made sure to confirm the desperate need to continue praying this way until the forgiveness goes from something you have to do, and becomes something you're grateful for. Freedom comes from a place of bondage. Break. Those. Chains, sister!

> *"14 For if you forgive men their trespasses, your heavenly Father will also forgive you. 15 But if you do not forgive men their trespasses, neither will your Father forgive your trespasses." (Matthew 6:14-15 NKJV)*

THE RESULT

Jesus says that *"peacemakers shall be called the children of God,"* because they become His children in His Kingdom family; his or her character resembles their Almighty Father. A child of God is one who not only carries on the family name but bears the family resemblance and reputation. Jesus is saying that as his followers become known as peacemakers, they will be recognized as the children of God because they share his name and share his mission. When we manifest the peace of Jesus to our families, friends, enemies, at church and to the world, God is proud to call us his "children".

WRITE Hebrews 2:11 in the space below.

_____

_____

_____

_____

Peacemaking efforts don't guarantee peace-achieving results. But we must keep at it and work for peace, prayerful that the barriers standing between us and our enemies are overcome, but never risk abandoning your devotion to God. We have to stand firm, no matter how much animosity and hostility we elicit from others, knowing that our obedience and message of love is what God desires. Whether the outcome is peace or persecution is God's business, not ours.

Jesus begins the Sermon on the Mount with the Beatitudes-- the most accurate descriptions of Godly characteristics, according to Jesus, to be attained in order to enter Heaven. The Beatitudes exemplify the features that describe the heavenly **dispositions** leading to our sanctification. The very end of the Sermon on the Mount is as compelling as the beginning, affirming the importance of the Beatitudes. His longest and most gripping sermon ends with the promise that anyone who lives in disobedience to the Beatitudes and of the Sermon on the Mount will be left standing in judgement on Judgement Day.

Matthew 7:26-27 (NIV)

"26 But everyone who hears these words of mine and does not put them into practice is like a foolish man who built his house on sand. 27 The rain came down, the streams rose, and the winds blew and beat against that house, and it fell with a great crash."

If we don't receive *mercy*, we will receive judgement. If we don't have hearts that are pure, we will never see God. And if we refuse to work at *making peace*, will never be called *children of God*. The Apostle Paul's letters almost always begin with the greeting *"Grace to you and peace from God our Father and the Lord Jesus Christ" (Phil. 1:2)*. Paul's epistles never reverse the order of "grace and peace." Grace always comes before peace because we have to experience the grace of God before we can experience the peace of God.

Christ teaches us divine lessons from God's own heart in how to bring peace in our hearts, our relationships, our church, our nation, and our world. Christ's call to peacemaking demands a radical paradigm shift in the world around us. If we are to be called daughters of God, then we must commit ourselves to the spiritual paradigm Jesus set forth for us to model.

We have to come into relationship with God through his son Jesus Christ before we can begin making peace with others. We have to know peace ourselves before we can make peace in our relationships. In other words, we can't make peace if we don't have peace. Will it be easy to make peace with everyone? No. Will we always experience a peaceful result in our efforts? No. Why, then should we really put forth so much hard work and effort if we aren't guaranteed a peaceful outcome? Because Jesus said so. In this life, you will have trouble, Jesus said, but in the midst of it all, we can have peace that surpasses all understanding—God's peace—IF we're willing to work for it every moment of our lives using the gifts we're given.

In Matthew 5:9, *"Blessed are the peacemakers for they are the children of God,"* St. Augustine (in A.D. 383) clarifies that *"where there is no contention, there is perfect peace. And because nothing can contend against God, the children of God are peacemakers."* The Peacemakers of God are the opposite of the peacemakers of the world, for the men of the world cry "peace, peace when there is no peace." St. Augustine explains that *"man is unable to rule over the lower things unless he in turn submits to the rule of a higher being. And this is the peace promised on earth to men of good will."* God's peace is only possible when everything is in its proper order and oriented to Him.

The Beatitudes are the heavenly norms for which we must strive to conform ourselves by cooperating with the graces gifted by the Holy Spirit. Christ presents the Beatitudes to us in their proper order from the lowest to the highest. The first step of the climb on this stairway to heaven is humility leading upwards through the rest of the Beatitudes towards the final end of wisdom. The Beatitudes embody the properly ordered mystical hierarchy of the rise to sanctity.

> On the other hand, if the unbelieving spouse walks out, you've got to let him or her go. You don't have to hold on desperately. God has called us to make the best of it, as peacefully as we can. You never know, wife: The way you handle this might bring your husband not only back to you but to God. You never know, husband: The way you handle this might bring your wife not only back to you but to God.
>
> 1 Corinthians 7:15-16 (MSG)

DISCUSSION

1. How does today's lesson impact you regarding a relationship that is strained due to conflict?

2. Do you feel like God is convincing you to initiate peace if you haven't already?

3. Have you have attempted to make peace with the someone you're at odds with but have been unsuccessful? Do you now have a deeper understanding of *their need* of your prayers for them?

4. Does today's lesson give you a new understanding of the importance of being a peacemaker?

5. What are changes you must make within yourself to become a peacemaker?

DAY 1

MATTHEW 5:43-47

_____

_____

_____

_____

_____

_____

_____

_____

_____

_____

_____

_____

_____

DAY 2

COLOSSIANS 1:19-20

_____

_____

_____

_____

_____

_____

_____

_____

_____

_____

_____

_____

_____

_____

DAY 3

MATTHEW 10:34-39

_____

_____

_____

_____

_____

_____

_____

_____

_____

_____

_____

_____

_____

_____

_____

DAY 4

EPHESIANS 2:15

_____

_____

_____

_____

_____

_____

_____

_____

_____

_____

_____

_____

_____

_____

_____

DAY 5

HEBREWS 12:14

_____

_____

_____

_____

_____

_____

_____

_____

_____

_____

_____

_____

_____

_____

Lesson 8

*Blessed are those who are persecuted for
righteousness' sake,
For theirs is the kingdom of heaven.*

Matthew 5:10 (NKJV)

The first three weeks of this study revealed the need to empty of self in order to be filled with God; dying of self, a divine emptiness that's a result of repentance and humility.

- *Matthew 5:3 Blessed are the poor in spirit, for theirs is the Kingdom of Heaven.*

- *Matthew 5:4 Blessed are those who mourn, for they will be comforted.*

- *Matthew 5:5 Blessed are the meek, for they will inherit the earth.*

Then in week 4, a shift began and your desires changed. An insatiable hunger and thirst for righteousness to remain living in total alignment with God.

- *Matthew 5:6 Blessed are those who hunger and thirst for righteousness, for they will be filled.*

The spiritual paradigm shift emerges and the transformation impacts everyone around you. The righteousness, longed for deep within, was revealed outwardly. From the depths of your soul, Jesus was displayed as you began to extend mercy, purity, and peacemaking to others.

- *Matthew 5:7 Blessed are the merciful, for they will be shown mercy.*

- *Matthew 5:8 Blessed are the pure in heart, for they will see God.*

- *Matthew 5:9 Blessed are the peacemakers, for they will be called children of God.*

The hunger will only be satisfied by extending what you, yourself have received—unending mercy, a pure heart, and a power to make peace. This is where the spiritual paradigm shift began.

The spiritual paradigm shift that occurs in the lives of those living in accordance with the beatitudes, both inwardly and outwardly, manifests and results in one's renewed character. The Beatitude this week is the final piece of the *'blessed are those who'* puzzle. Jesus knew that God required His disciples to live righteously and gave them a detailed description of the paradigm they were to follow. He did this because He knew the suffering they were going to face for the sake of the Gospel.

The condition of those who are blessed in this Beatitude is the same condition as those who were hungry and thirsty in week 4—their *righteousness*. However, this time Jesus addresses those who are persecuted and afflicted for the sake of righteousness. The NLT version of Matthew 5:10 states, *"God blesses those who are persecuted for doing right, for the Kingdom of Heaven is theirs."* Righteousness means doing the right thing according to God.

The Apostle Paul's second letter to the Corinthians contains more autobiographical material than any of his other writings. He was furious with the members of the church in Corinth and Christians throughout Acacia. A group of men who turned out to be false teachers, had come to Corinth and began wreaking havoc among the members by presenting themselves as apostles. The men were challenging, among other things, Paul's personal integrity and his authority as an apostle. Paul decided to make a quick trip to Corinth in hopes of remedying this situation. The visit didn't go as he'd planned. He dearly loved the members of this church and they persecuted him, choosing to trust in the false teachings of the men who'd slithered in and turned everything upside down. This was very painful for Paul. When Paul returned to Ephesus, he wrote the Corinthians this severe letter *"out of great distress and anguish of heart and with many tears" (2 Corinthians 2:4 NKJV).*

Paul was struck down and persecuted every day of his life as an apostle of Jesus Christ. His suffering was relentless, much like ours and our children's. Paul's suffering was for the sake of spreading the Gospel.

READ 2 Corinthians 4:8-12. WRITE verses 8 and 9 below.

_____

_____

_____

_____

_____

_____

Paul suffered for Jesus' sake and desperately wanted the members of the church to understand that the life of an apostle would be difficult. I love The Message translation of what Paul said next, "[13-15] *We're not keeping this quiet, not on your life. Just like the psalmist who wrote, 'I believed it, so I said it,' we say what we believe. And what we believe is that the One who raised up the Master Jesus will just as certainly raise us up with you, alive. Every detail works to your advantage and to God's glory: more and more grace, more and more people, more and more praise!" (2 Corinthians 4:13-15 MSG).*

I BELIEVED THEREFORE I SPOKE! We pray because we believe in God and we believe that He hears our prayers. When we pray in our suffering it's further proof of our belief that God sees our suffering, the suffering of our children, and our trust that He is with us. Our eternal life is dependent on our belief! The suffering we endure on a daily basis is our passion, our salvation. Our suffering as a result of our children's suffering requires us to be focused on God and our constant need for Him. Grace is spreading to more and more people so that they'll "give thanks" to "abound the glory of God."

READ 2 Corinthians 4:16-18

1. Paul has an interesting view of aging, suffering, and what matters most while were here on earth. WRITE verse 18 in your own words.

Sometimes we feel as though we'll never find rest. Sometimes we are left wondering what "normal" feels like in regards to a family unit. By our complete submission and trust in God, we pray relentlessly, which renews our spirits and relationship with Him. *Momentary, light affliction* is what most suffer; ours, however, is not momentary. Our children's suffering is far from momentary or light.

Verse 18, "*So we fix our eyes* <u>not</u> *on what is seen, but* <u>on what is</u> *unseen, since* <u>what is seen</u> *is* <u>temporary</u>, *but* <u>what is unseen</u> *is* <u>eternal,</u>" is a direct reflection of Matthew 25:35-40.

> [35] For I was hungry, and <u>you gave Me</u> *something* to eat;
> I was thirsty, and <u>you gave Me</u> *something* to drink;
> I was a stranger, and <u>you invited Me in</u>;
> [36] naked, and <u>you clothed Me</u>;
> I was sick, and <u>you visited Me</u>;
> I was in prison, and <u>you came to Me</u>.'
> [37] Then the <u>righteous</u> will answer Him, 'Lord, <u>when did we see You</u> hungry, and feed You, or thirsty, and give You *something* to drink?
> [38] And <u>when did we see You</u> a stranger, and invite You in, or naked, and clothe You?
> [39] <u>When did we see You</u> sick, or in prison, and come to You?'
> [40] The King will answer and say to them, 'Truly I say to you, to the extent that <u>you did it to one of these brothers of Mine, even the least</u> *of them,* <u>you did it to Me</u>.'
>
> (*Matthew 25:35-40 NASB*)

<u>SEEN:</u> (Matthew 25:35-36)

- Jesus tells them that when they **saw** that He needed help, they met his needs and helped Him. The afflictions were *temporary*—hungry, thirsty, homeless, naked, sick, and imprisoned.

<u>UNSEEN:</u> (Matthew 25: 37-39)

- This makes no sense to the people He's talking to. They indeed helped those in need, but they **never saw Jesus** anywhere.

<u>ETERNAL:</u> (Matthew 25:40)

- Jesus explains that HE WAS THE RECIPIENT of their mercy; they were in the presence of the Lord every single time they helped those who couldn't help themselves. The Kingdom of Heaven, **eternal life**, was theirs as a result of their mercy and sacrifice.

This is exactly what Paul is talking about in 2 Corinthians 18! "*So we fix our eyes <u>not</u> on what is seen, but <u>on what is</u> unseen, since <u>what is seen is</u> temporary, but <u>what is unseen is</u> eternal.*"

Just because you don't see healing in our children TODAY, I promise you that GOD HEALS! You might or might not see your child walk, run, jump, skip, hop, ride a bike, drive a car, go to prom, or graduate from college in this life. You might or might not hold a conversation with your child in this life. BUT YOU WILL SEE YOUR CHILD HEALED AND PERFECT IN HEAVEN! Please don't miss this! Hear me when I say that it is 100% guaranteed, promised, freely given by the blood of Jesus Christ on the Cross that YOUR CHILD WILL BE HEALED!!! If you want to experience life with them in their perfect state then you must deny yourself and take up your cross and follow Jesus. It's ONLY through your salvation that you and your child be whole. Your child will be in Heaven and you DO NOT WANT TO MISS ETERNITY WITH THEM!

Paul is telling us in 2 Corinthians 4:18 that the things we can see (experience in the here and now) are temporary; the things which are not seen (Jesus looking back at us in the eyes of our children) are eternal. As long as we're on earth, our afflictions weigh us down, but they're producing for us an eternal glory that will lift us up higher than we could've ever imagined!

Because God's children are living right in His eyes, doing everything in accordance to His will and desires, their lives convict others who are living in darkness. When we grasp the reality of persecution, we can avoid being blind-sided by harsh words, insults, judgement, and rejection. As Christians living in a world filled with non-believers, we will face condemnation and persecution. What matters most is that we remain focused on the Kingdom of Heaven.

The Apostle Paul endured

- Suffering and persecution day in and day out as a result of his unwavering commitment to living righteously.

- Suffering for the Gospel, resulting in eminent danger everywhere he went.

- Suffered for the ministry, resulting in constant attempts from outsiders to destroy and disband churches that were formed by his ministry.

WRITE 2 Corinthians 5:7 in the space below.

_____

_____

_____

_____

DISCUSSION

1. Do you feel persecuted at times due to the lack of acceptance of your child because of their disability?

2. How difficult is it to trust in the unseen versus the things you can see (i.e. healing, language, behavior improvement, emotional improvement)?

3. Do you feel intimidated by the spiritual disposition requirements Jesus details in the Beatitudes? If so, which one(s)? Why do you feel that way?

4. What is the Holy Spirit saying to you in this lesson?

5. Do you pray with your child at night? If not, please start tonight.

**While journaling this week, write about times in your life (as a child, a teen, and adult) when you felt afflicted by persecution from someone. Begin with the moment it happened, then who it was that hurt you, and the issues it created for you emotionally and spiritually. Pray to begin healing the pain and forgiveness for the one who hurt you.

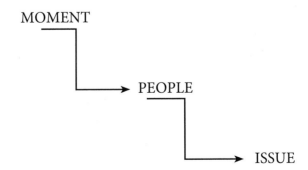

DAY 1

JEREMIAH 29:13

_____

_____

_____

_____

_____

_____

_____

_____

_____

_____

_____

_____

_____

DAY 2

2 Corinthians 4:13

_____

_____

_____

_____

_____

_____

_____

_____

_____

_____

_____

_____

_____

_____

DAY 3

JOHN 3:19-20

_____

_____

_____

_____

_____

_____

_____

_____

_____

_____

_____

_____

_____

DAY 4

1 CORINTHIANS 2:14

DAY 5

2 CORINTHIANS 13:5

_____

_____

_____

_____

_____

_____

_____

_____

_____

_____

_____

_____

_____

_____

Lesson 9

²⁴"But woe to you who are rich,
for you have already received your comfort.
²⁵ Woe to you who are well fed now,
for you will go hungry.
Woe to you who laugh now,
for you will mourn and weep.

Luke 6:24-25 (NIV)

Before I began writing this study of the Beatitudes, I assumed I knew what the conditions and results were, and the direction each lesson would take. I thought that being *"poor in spirit"* meant being devastated, that being *"meek"* would speak into our weakness or timidity, and that being *"pure in heart"* was another way of saying someone was simply very nice. I was beautifully mistaken.

What I learned verse after verse, hour after hour, and day after day while studying from the crack of dawn and resuming late at night after my kids were asleep, was that GOD'S WISDOM and MY EARTHLY WAY OF THINKING are incomparable. I already loved reading the Bible, but this has shown me that the poignant layers of God and Jesus' intentional and eternal teachings are <u>impossible</u> to interpret by simply reading the words on the fragile pages. In order to grow in understanding and write what God intended this study to become, I'd need to take myself out of the equation. The Holy Spirit, prayer, obedience, patience, along with commentaries, and researching wisdom written by generations of Apostolic teachings from Biblical scholars and theologians guided my work. God knew that if He'd shown me how little I knew *before* embarking on this journey, my fear would've stopped me from experiencing Him and His majesty. Kingdom work is always met with doubt and attacks from the enemy. As my friend and mentor Francine Ivey says, "You don't want to win a battle, but lose the war."

We don't have the ability to glance at a scripture once or twice and receive what God is saying to us through the words on paper. We can't reevaluate ourselves based on what *we* think Jesus expects of us, and this was proven week after week, Beatitude after Beatitude. This week we're wrapping up our study of the Beatitudes with the Sermon on the Plains in Luke 6. The importance of this particular sermon is the combination Jesus teaches of blessings and woes—and they are completely contrary to what those who were present when He preached expected to hear Him to say.

As William Barclay stated, "The challenge of the Beatitude is, 'Will you be happy in the world's way, or in Christ's way?" (*The Daily Study Bible, Luke, p.77*)

Jesus preached the Beatitudes in two separate sermons, The Sermon on the Mount in Matthew 5 and the Sermon on the Plains in Luke 6. Unlike the Sermon on the Mount, the four Beatitudes that He preached in Luke 6 are followed by four "*woes*". The *woes* are warnings of God's explosive displeasure for those whose current lives seem extremely fortunate to the outside world. However, their worldly comforts blind them; their ignorance and/or selfishness called out by Jesus Himself. His admonishments are strong and their unwillingness to recognize or appreciate the real values of God's kingdom will have severe repercussions. Their present conditions are fleeting and Jesus wants them to repent before it's too late.

POOR VS. RICH

Luke 6:20, 24 (NABRE)

[20] *And turning His gaze toward His disciples, He began* to say, "Blessed *are* you *who are* poor, for yours is the kingdom of God. [24] *But woe to you who are rich, for you are receiving your comfort in full.*

Those who live in poverty would probably disagree with Jesus when He says they're blessed. I'm sure wealthy people would never equate being poor with being blessed. But Jesus is teaching a different kind of wealth, something that's far more valuable than monetary wealth. Throughout the Gospels, Jesus clearly draws a line that divides Kingdom values and the world's values; two groups of people and there is absolutely no middle ground.

READ Matthew 6:19-21 and SUMMARIZE it in your own words.

_____

_____

_____

_____

_____

The poor people of the New Testament times never rejected Jesus; it was always the rich religious establishment that resisted Him and His teachings. The poor, the sick, the blind, the lame, the broken sinners, and the dying were always forced to trust in God. They had nothing of worldly value; therefore, they had everything in Christ. Their faith is what filled their needs, resulting in abundant treasures that await them in Heaven. It's the same today as it was back then according to God—true wealth is measured in the desire for both emptiness of self and hunger and thirst for Jesus.

READ Matthew 6:24

1. How many masters can one person serve?

2. Why?

Mammon is an Aramaic word that means "riches". In the biblical sense of the word, mammon is the spirit that's placed on money, resulting in a person's trust and faith resting in money. God demands we place our trust and faith in HIM, so if our trust and faith is placed in anything other than God Himself, we're actually worshipping the spirit of something OTHER THAN GOD. That's why Jesus says we can't serve two masters; we will either love the one and hate the other or be loyal to one and despise the other. Jesus isn't saying that having money or wealth is a bad thing. In his book, *The Blessed Life*, Pastor Robert Morris explains the difference between blessed money and cursed money-

> "Money that is submitted to God and His purposes has the Spirit of God on it—which is why it multiplies and cannot be consumed by the devourer. I'm convinced that money that has been submitted to God—wealth that is devoted to serving Him rather than trying to replace Him—is blessed by God. In a very real sense, God's Spirit blesses it.
>
> On the other hand, money that is not submitted to God has the spirit of mammon on it by default. That's why people so often try to use money to control or manipulate others. Its why people think money can bring them happiness and fulfillment."
>
> *(The Blessed Life, p.52)*

The saying, *"the rich keep getting richer, and the poor keep getting poorer"* was definitely spoken by someone with a spirit of mammon. You can look at both sides and see the idolatry of money, either from the poor person who hungered to be rich or the rich person who coveted their wealth. Either way, there's no place for God. One side loves money; the other side does, too.

When people but their faith in money, they trust that it will solve all their problems. Where is God in that scenario? That actually shows more about someone's lack of faith in God, so much so that they trust a spirit who is the exact opposite of God. They're leaving God completely out of their lives, resulting in discontentment because they'll never find happiness or fulfillment.

Blessed are the poor and the poor in spirit. God can't fill what is full; a spirit that is filled with mammon will never make room for God. God will provide an empty spirit with Himself, leaving nothing be desired except His love, His joy, His happiness, His provision, and the overflowing blood of His Son, Jesus Christ.

So, where your treasure is, there your heart will be also *(Matthew 6:21)* because *the love of* money is the root of all kinds of evil *(1 Timothy 6:10)*. The love is what matters—the love you have for God. You'll never be as rich as you are when your faith and trust are in God and God alone. Money isn't the root of all kinds of evil—***the love of money*** is.

WRITE 1 Timothy 6:10 in your own words in the space below.

_____

_____

_____

_____

_____

_____

HUNGRY VS. WELL-FED

Luke 6:21a, 25a (NASB)

21a *Blessed are you who hunger now, for you shall be satisfied.*
25 a *Woe to you who are well-fed now, for you shall be hungry.*

We learned that *those who hunger and thirst for righteousness will be filled* in week 4 of this study; hunger and thirst tell of a want within. Jesus speaks of this hunger and thirst in The Parable of the Great Banquet (Luke 14 16-23). Jesus described a man hosting a lavish dinner party, but when the dinner was ready to be served, the guests were busy doing what they wanted to do and excused themselves. That's when the host sent his servant out to bring the poor, the crippled, the blind, and the lame. Jesus tells us that we are to invite the less fortunate to our table; we are to bless those who will never be able to repay us.

This woe is similar to the first. Since righteousness is the true soul food, those who are satiated by the things of this world right now will be left ultimately empty. The Bible's book of Ecclesiastes was written by a very wealthy man who ultimately discovers that a life of luxury lived apart from God is meaninglessness. In Ecclesiastes 2:1-11, he details the many ways he used his money in hopes of fulfill his need for pleasure and happiness.

READ Ecclesiastes 2:1-11.

1. How did this man spend his money (*vs. 4-9*)?

2. When he took a step back and began looking at everything and done, everything his money allowed him to experience, how did he feel?

3. Was he serving God or mammon?

He had all the money in the world and used it to build homes and vineyards, gardens and parks. These were for HIS enjoyment, not to benefit the citizens who lived nearby. He also built reservoirs to water all of the trees so that he'd have the most delicious fruit to eat but he wasn't feeding the homeless, was he? He hired a full-service staff AND their children so that he'd never have to lift a finger. He bought livestock, silver, gold, and everything that a King would have because they represented wealth. His parties were lavish, and he hired only the best of both men and women entertainers. Oh, and don't forget about the *harem* of lovers at his beck and call.

He lived like a celebrity all right! He denied himself nothing, and indulged in whatever he wanted. Yet he realizes that none of it truly satisfied him. He was well-fed, yet starving. Seeking pleasure turned out to be meaningless and left him empty. The world we live in is a gluttonous world—*more, more, more.* If only the world knew that the best life is lived by those who are empty of self and filled with God's imputed righteousness. God can't fill what is full, especially a bank account filled with the Spirit of Mammon.

Then Jesus declared, "I am the bread of life.
Whoever comes to me will never go hungry,
and whoever believes in me will never be thirsty."

John 6:35 (NIV)

WEEPING VS. LAUGHING

Luke 6:21b, 25b (NIV)

21b Blessed are you who weep now, for you will laugh.
25b Woe to you who laugh now, for you will mourn and weep.

In our lives as moms of special needs children, we spend quite a lot of time crying. For some, it's the fragility of the disability, for others it's the overwhelming chaos. Regardless of the special need, it hurts our hearts. This Beatitude may not give you much comfort if you simply read it, but I pray you receive Jesus' words in a much deeper way today.

In John chapter 11, Jesus raises a man named Lazarus from the dead. Jesus adored Lazarus and his two sisters, Mary and Martha whose family lived in the village of Bethany, about two miles east of Jerusalem. When Lazarus fell ill, Mary and Martha sent word to Jesus about their brother in hopes that He'd immediately return to heal him.

READ John 11:1-16.

1. When Jesus was told Lazarus was gravely ill, how did He respond?

2. How long after hearing news of Lazarus' decline in health did Jesus remain where He was?

3. Knowing how much Jesus loved Lazarus and his sisters, does Jesus' lack of urgency to return immediately make sense to you? Why or why not?

4. WRITE verse 16 in the space below.

_____

_____

_____

_____

_____

_____

Jesus' disciples were worried about returning to Judea because the last time they were there the Jews tried to stone him, but Jesus wasn't. His disciples continue to voice concern, adding that if Lazarus is asleep, he will get better because they thought Lazarus was truly sleeping. What Jesus knew that His disciples didn't was that Lazarus was dead. Once Jesus tells them about Lazarus' passing, they all agree to return with Him.

READ John 11:17-27

By the time Jesus returned, Lazarus had been gone for four days. When Martha came to Jesus, she immediately says, *"If you'd been here, my brother wouldn't have died."* I'm sure Martha's statement hits home for you, doesn't it? Have you felt this way towards God? Have you struggled with your faith, losing much of your belief because of the unanswered prayers for your child's healing? Do you wonder if Jesus hears your prayers? Have you given up hope, resolving yourself to believe that He's turned a blind eye to the inward suffering you and your family goes through as a result of your child's chronic suffering? Martha didn't. READ verse 22 again.

Martha immediately follows that statement with another that is not to be overlooked, *"But I know that even now God will give you whatever you ask."* Her faith was shaken, but not destroyed. What mattered most to Jesus was that her *belief* outweighed her *pain.*

WHAT IF = Fear

EVEN IF = Faith

Jesus tells Martha that her brother will rise again and she agrees, knowing that everyone rises from the dead on the day of Judgement, but that's not what Jesus means. He says to her, *"I am the resurrection and the life. The* <u>one who believes in me will live</u>, *even though they die; and* <u>whoever lives by believing in me will never die</u>. *Do you believe this?"*

WRITE verse 27 in the space below in your own words.

_____

_____

_____

_____

_____

_____

READ John 11:28-35

There are only three times in scripture where we're told Jesus wept. John 11:35 tells us Jesus wept for the first time when He asked where Lazarus' body was buried. Those two words, the shortest verse in the Bible, are profound.

Another record of Jesus weeping is referenced in *Hebrews 5:7* where Paul refers to Jesus weeping in the Garden of Gethsemane the night before His arrest and crucifixion in *Matthew 26:36-39*. The third time in *Luke 19:37-41* describes the intense scene that caused Jesus to weep for the third time, upon His triumphal entry into Jerusalem on the donkey, palm branches laid out on the road for Him by cheering crowds. The sounds of so many people rejoicing and crying out, *"Blessed is the King who comes in the name of the Lord!"* This angered the Pharisees that were there, and they shouted at Jesus to rebuke the disciples but He refuses, saying, *"I tell you, if they keep quiet, the stones will cry out."* As he crests the top of the Mount of Olives, Jesus sees the city spread out before Him. Overwhelmed by grief, He began to cry for those below, those who would never experience eternal life.

That day in Bethany, some of the Jews who were present assumed Jesus was crying because of His love for Lazarus and being devastated by his passing. Others who were there wondered what took Him so long, silently blaming Jesus for Lazarus' death because He took so long to get there. When Jesus, Mary, Martha, and the other people who were there arrived at the tomb where Lazarus had been for four days, Jesus tells them to take away the stone at the entrance. This is where broken faith meets disbelief, resulting in God doing what only God can do.

READ John 11:38-44

This story about Jesus raising Lazarus from the dead epitomizes BOTH the blessing and the woe in Luke 6:21b and 25b. Mary and Martha were undoubtedly filled with joy and laughter when their beloved brother came back to life! They wept, but only for a few days.

What's even more powerful is the underlying reflection of the woe for *"those who laugh now, for you will mourn and weep."* There was a reason Jesus waited so long before returning to Bethany where Lazarus succumbed to his sickness. Jesus knew that there would be numerous non-believers who would come to comfort the sisters in their time of grief. He knew that these people would need to see a God-sized miracle in order to change their beliefs; a God-sized miracle so big that they wouldn't be able to deny that Jesus was the Son of God, the Messiah. I can't think of a more shocking, fantastical way to prove that Jesus was who He said He was! The lost souls who were standing near the tomb witnessed Jesus raise a man from the dead—four days after his death. There were lives saved that day, eternal lives. God knows some people need to witness a Lazarus-sized miracle in order for them to give their lives to Him. Jesus knew He had to wait so that those who doubted would no longer be able to deny.

DISCUSSION

1. How do you feel now about money after learning what's at risk in being monetarily rich for a moment on earth versus being poor in spirit which leads to eternal life filled with treasures in Heaven?

2. Is there someone you feel led to pray for regarding what you've learned today about the Spirit of Mammon?

3. Does being hungry now feel like a blessing after learning God's promise that you will be beyond full for eternity as a daughter of the King of Kings?

4. Do you resonate with any of the people in the lessons today? Who and why?

5. What if = _____   Even if = _____

DAY 1

ISAIAH 3:10-11

_____

_____

_____

_____

_____

_____

_____

_____

_____

_____

_____

_____

_____

_____

DAY 2

ECCLESIASTES 10:16-17

_____

_____

_____

_____

_____

_____

_____

_____

_____

_____

_____

_____

_____

_____

DAY 3

PSALM 119:36

_____

_____

_____

_____

_____

_____

_____

_____

_____

_____

_____

_____

_____

_____

DAY 4

PHILIPIANS 3:19

_____

_____

_____

_____

_____

_____

_____

_____

_____

_____

_____

_____

_____

_____

DAY 5

2 CORINTHIANS 5:7

_____

_____

_____

_____

_____

_____

_____

_____

_____

_____

_____

_____

_____

_____

Lesson 10

> ²²"Blessed are you when people hate you and when they exclude you and revile you and spurn your name as evil, on account of the Son of Man! ²³Rejoice in that day, and leap for joy, for behold, your reward is great in heaven; for so their fathers did to the prophets.
>
> ²⁶"Woe to you, when all people speak well of you, for so their fathers did to the false prophets.
>
> Luke 6:22-23, 26 (ASV)

Hatred for Christians is nothing new. The Christian faith has been under constant persecution and judgement from the secular world since Jesus began His ministry. In Matthew 5:10-11, Jesus says, *"Blessed are* those who are persecuted for righteousness' sake, for theirs is the kingdom of heaven. Blessed are you when they revile and persecute *you, and say all kinds of evil against you falsely for My sake."* The Beatitude in Luke differs with Jesus adding, *"when men hate you."* Why are these four words so important?

HATED VS. PRAISED

HATE FOR THE 12

READ Luke 20-23

Though there were huge crowds around Him, Jesus directs these particular blessings to the twelve apostles He'd chosen right before this sermon began

(Luke 6:20). Jesus knew the repercussions they would later suffer for following Him. The apostle's conversion from Judaism to the early church would result in their automatic expulsion or excommunication from the Jewish synagogue.

The Apostles played significant roles in building God's Kingdom, but it was going to come at a huge cost and Jesus was ensuring their awareness of what they were up against—exclusion, persecution, reproach, and suffering they'd face as apostles of Jesus Christ. "Christian," from the Greek *Christianos*, was originally a derogatory term used by non-believers (Greeks and Romans) to describe the followers of Jesus Christ as slaves. The term "Christians" had never been used until the church braced it as its own in Antioch (Acts 11:26).

They'd all separated from their former religions to become Christians. Jesus knew that the Pharisees and Jews would refuse to accept a Christian faith, rejecting anyone who called themselves disciples of Christ.

The blessing in this Beatitude is promised <u>only</u> to those who endured the persecution, hatred, rejection, and isolation for Christ's sake. Their refusal to seek popularity and acceptance from the world would place them in the same league as the prophets of the Old Testament such as Elijah, Isaiah, Jeremiah, Ezekiel, and Daniel. Being a prophet was never easy and many of them were killed as a result of their faithful obedience to God, which is why they hold a position of honor in Heaven.

READ 1 Peter 2:11-12

1. What was Peter's warning in verse 11?

2. By living an honest life and standing firm in their faith, what did Peter say would happen if they were ever accused of wrongdoing?

3. Who is the ultimate judge of right and wrong?

THE PRAISED

Luke 6:26 (NKJV)

Woe to you when all men speak well of you,
For so did their fathers to the false prophets.

The desire to be accepted and loved is part of our nature as human beings. The physical need for acceptance begins at birth, proven by the silencing of a newborn's cry the moment they're held in the arms of their mother. Our longing to belong never stops. Children want to be liked, teenagers want to be popular, and adults struggle with rejection.

These days, people are literally determining their worth based on how many "likes" and "shares" they get on social media. Many videos that go viral are intended to spread hate and discontent, dividing countries and cultures. This proves that even those filled with hate want to be accepted.

In John 15, Jesus is telling the apostles that they must seek faithfulness, not popularity, because popularity is based on false values—worldly values, not Kingdom values.

READ John 15:18-19

1. Why does the world hate those who follow Christ?

The spirit of rejection is a demonic spirit, and it's one of the most common demonic strongholds in the world today. This demonic spirit attacks the identity of the person, destroying their self-esteem, working overtime to destroy who they are and their Kingdom purpose in life. The enemy is invading the souls of God's children because he wants to silence a person's ability to hear God's voice.

READ John 15:20-25

1. Why will the apostles be persecuted?

2. Those who persecute disciples of Jesus do so because they do not know the _____ who _____ Jesus (*verse 21*)?

3. True or false: It's possible to hate Jesus but love God.

4. What was their reason for hating Jesus in verse 25? Why do you feel they hated Jesus?

Persecution is a growing tree whose stems are a product of rooted hate. In John 15:5, Jesus says that those who are not living branches of the vine of Jesus Christ are helpless and defenseless, *"I am the vine; you are the branches. If you remain in me and I in you, you will bear much fruit; apart from Me you can do nothing"* (NIV). Jesus was proof that living to please God, even if it results in death, is what matters most.

- Apart from Jesus, what can you do? _____

Jesus never sought praise from the people who followed Him. His desire was to glorify God, not Himself. He was greatly praised by those in a crowd who cried out, *"Hosanna! Blessed is He who comes in the name of the Lord!"* (*Mark 11:9 NIV*), but a week later that same crowd was screaming, *"Crucify Him!"* (*Mark 15:14 NIV*). Jesus never placed His faith and trust in those who claimed to love Him; He didn't want His disciples to misplace their trust and faith either.

READ John 12:27-36

1. What happened when Jesus cried out to God in verse 28?

2. Who heard God's response?

3. Who was supposed to benefit from God's thunderous reply?

4. WRITE verses 35-36 in your own words.

_____

_____

_____

_____

_____

Those who heard the voice of God, words spoken TO THEM and FOR THEM, still refused to believe! They'd seen Jesus perform miracle after miracle and many signs but that wasn't enough. They were placing their faith in what they thought "forever" meant, what they'd been told it meant.

READ John 12:37-41

Jesus wasn't trying to turn their disbelief into belief. He wasn't mad or resentful that they'd refused to accept Him as the Son of God. Jesus knew it would be *impossible* for them to believe at this time; the day they'd come to accept that He was who He said He was would come later—the day of His resurrection. This was, unbeknownst to the unbelievers in the crowd, fulfilling prophesy from the Old Testament Prophet, Isaiah.

READ John 12:42-50

1. Why did many of the leaders keep their belief in Jesus to themselves?

2. Whose praise did they care most about?

3. By believing in Jesus, who else do you believe in?

4. What happens to someone who lives in agony and angst once they believe in Jesus?

5. Who is the judge? _____

    Who is the Savior? _____

When we live for the approval of the world, we lose God's approval. The line that Jesus draws for us, separating worldly values and Kingdom values can't be crossed. We can't have one foot on both sides. The full spectrum of the spiritual paradigm shift is revealed when we are placed by GOD, gently set with both feet on the ground on the Kingdom side of the line!

We can jump for joy when we're persecuted and rejected as a result of our love for Jesus! And, because we're empty of self and filled with God's righteousness, we won't hesitate to stand firm when others revile and mock us because of our faith. Our adversaries on the other side of the line can't hurt us as long as we're children of God living with BOTH feet firmly planted on the Kingdom side of the line. It's impossible for those living in darkness to cross a line they don't see. Without light, they're blind and unable to see due to the total darkness that surrounds them.

Centurions were commanders of centuries (100 legionaries) in the ancient Roman army. Julius Caesar is said to have promoted the Centurions in his army for displays of valor. There was a Centurion who stood by Jesus, guarding Him, and witnessed every moment as He hung on the cross. This strong, powerful warrior watched Jesus suffer. This high-ranking official was the first to believe that Jesus really was the Son of God, and the timing of his revelation is extraordinary.

READ Mark 15:34-39

In verse 39, the brave centurion, captain of the squad guarding Jesus, realized that of the many men he'd seen die in the past, Jesus' death was different. Even the most seasoned soldier is blind, incapable of seeing what he refuses to believe until God reveals Himself. Guilty men rarely lift up prayer for those who'd persecuted them.

In Luke23, as He hung on the cross, Jesus lifts up a prayer of forgiveness—this forgiveness was for the benefit of those who'd hung Him there to die. The first words Jesus spoke upon the cross were to God on behalf of those who hated Him enough to kill Him. *"Then Jesus said, 'Father, forgive them, for they know not what they do.'" (Luke 23:34).* Jesus never did anything to glorify Himself. Torture and crucifixion weren't enough to shake the divine fulfillment of the Old Testament; Jesus knew that God's work and God's will was what must be done.

As a mom, we suffer in seeing our children suffer. We also hurt when we see our children bullied, mocked, and rejected. We share in their pain when we are refused entrance through the doors of churches because they don't accept our families as we are. Jesus has given us the ultimate example of what we're to do when every part of our soul feels like unleashing a wrath of vengeance or anger. Jesus knew the people who were killing Him were children of God—they were imperfect and ignorant due to their unwillingness to accept what they did not know. It was their fear that drove them and Jesus' love that saved them. Without loving Jesus with all your heart, all your soul, and your entire mind, you'll miss living a life that's in alignment with Him—full of grace… for others.

I would like to end this study and our time together with the words Jesus spoke before taking His last breath. With these words, Jesus' suffering ended. With these words, yours will too.

Hatred caused Jesus' suffering, but it was His *love, God's love,* that allows us and our children the opportunity to live free of pain and in perfection with Him forever. God bless you, my beautiful, beautiful friend. Pray now, then WRITE Luke 23:46 in the space below.